MANY FURROWS

THE WAYFARER'S LIBRARY

MANY FURROWS

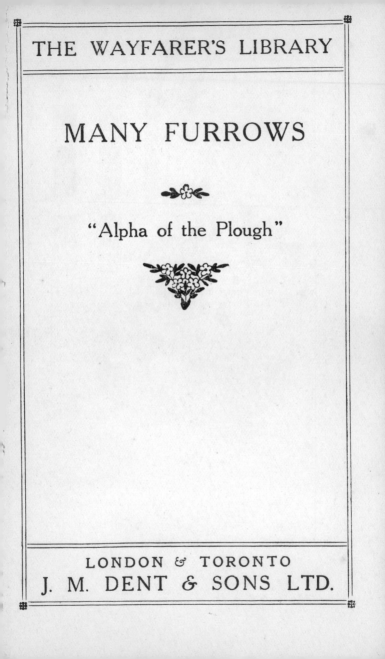

"Alpha of the Plough"

LONDON & TORONTO
J. M. DENT & SONS LTD.

First Published 1924
First Published in this Series . 1927

PRINTED IN GREAT BRITAIN

TO

MY WIFE

PREFACE

WHEN Benedick said that he would die a bachelor he did not know, as he observed later, that he would live to be married. In the same way, I have to confess that when in my preface to *Windfalls* I hinted that it would be the last of these little books, I did not think that there would be another.

Mr. Dent has convinced me of my mistake. This is the fourth collection I have made and, warned of the danger of forecasting the future, I will say no word in prejudice of a fifth. The essays, like those in the previous volumes, have appeared in *The Star*, many of them also in the *Manchester Evening News* and some in the *Glasgow Citizen*.

CONTENTS

Contents

MANY FURROWS

DREAM JOURNEYS

I HAD a singular dream last night. I found myself on Robinson Crusoe's Island and, curiously enough, in Robinson Crusoe's rôle. In the bright sunshine, by the sea-shore. I was turning over the stores of eatables, chiefly bags of potatoes, it seemed to me, that were lying about. There was abundance to go on with and I did not feel at all disturbed at the prospect of not being called for for many a long day. I was alone, but without the sense of solitude. Indeed, I was entirely happy and free from care. I feel, even now that I am awake, the glow of the warm sunshine and the peace of the sands and the sea. Most dreams are easily traceable to some waking circumstance, and this quite enjoyable spiritual experience was, I suppose, due to a conversation I had had about Honolulu and my regret that I was never likely to see the islands of the Pacific. The friendly spirit who has charge of my dreams evidently took the hint and wafted me away to Juan Fernandez. I am half-disposed, so pleasant is the memory, to regret that he did not leave me there, wrapped in immortal dreams of plenty, peace and sunshine.

I shall repeat the experiment of nudging my amiable

Dream Journeys

djinn into agreeable activity. I have a great many schemes to put before him, and if my friends discover that I am talking with enthusiasm about Pizarro they will know that I am putting in a plea with the director of dreams for a trip to Peru, and that if I am unusually concerned, even distressed, about the fate of Mummery, or the importance of conquering Mount Everest, I have in mind the possibility of a climbing excursion in the Himalayas. It is an excellent way of filling up the blanks in one's experience.

As we get on in years we become conscious of those blanks. We feel that we are in danger of missing much of the show we came to see. While we are young, say, up to fifty, we are not troubled. There seems plenty of time still to do everything worth doing, and see everything worth seeing. But after fifty the horizon shrinks most alarmingly, or perhaps it would be truer to say that it expands most alarmingly, and we find that, not only is Heaven, as Hood said, farther off than it seems in childhood, but that the desirable places of the earth have become more inaccessible. When I was a boy and had my imagination stirred by tales of the backwoods and Russell's songs about

> The land of the free
> Where the mighty Missouri rolls down to the sea,

I had no doubt that I should one day roll down with it, probably in a canoe, with a friendly Indian. Everything seemed possible then. Life was so enormously long an affair that the only disturbing thought was how you would be able to fill it up, and you had no

Dream Journeys

more idea of missing a trip up the Amazon or seeing the Rockies and Niagara and the Grand Cañon when you grew up than of not being privileged to smoke a pipe or to have a latchkey or to go to Lord's or the Oval and see Grace whenever you felt inclined.

In this comfortable conviction that we shall do everything in good time we jog along doing nothing in particular, getting more and more like the donkey we used to see at Carisbrooke Castle years ago, tramping round and round its tread-mill without ever reaching anywhere. We are not disquieted. We feel that any day in the infinite days before us we shall be threading the Thousand Islands or climbing the Heights of Abraham, or seeing the sunrise in the Oberland or the sunset in Venice, or the dawn coming up like thunder on the road to Mandalay, or standing in the Coliseum at Rome or among the ruins of Carthage or Timgad, or sailing among the isles of Greece or catching the spicy breezes that, according to the hymn of the good Bishop Heber, whom we could not suspect of romancing, come from Ceylon's favoured isle.

And so with other things. One day, assuredly, we shall take to horse-riding, and canter gaily round Rotten Row, or we shall go yachting in the Mediterranean or shooting in Scotland. And think of the books we shall read in the enormous leisure that lies before us. There is that fellow Karl Marx, for example. He certainly must be read—some day. It is absurd not to know what he said, when all the world goes on babbling so learnedly about him. No doubt he is a dull fellow, but we cannot, of course, leave the world

Dream Journeys

without knowing why he created such a hubbub. And there are a lot of other high-brows that we shall become acquainted with in good time. We shall really study those categorical imperatives of the illustrious Kant, and the monism of Spinoza, and the *Leviathan* and the *Novum Organum*, and a score of other solemn books that ought to be read and must be read—some day. We are not worried about these things. We have years and years before us, and shall need some stout fellows like these to make the time pass by.

That is how we drift until, somewhere in the fifties, we begin to suspect that we are cutting it rather fine, and that all those riches of experience that we confidently expected to enjoy and those intellectual conquests that we intended to make are slipping beyond our grasp. Karl Marx is still joyfully unthumbed, the *Novum Organum* still beckons us unavailingly from the abode where the eternal are, and we are still hazy about the categorical imperatives of the illustrious Kant. The call of the mighty Missouri falls faint on our ears, and Ceylon's spicy breezes we have to take at second-hand from the saintly Heber. We are chained to the No. 16 bus to Cricklewood or the tube to Shepherd's Bush, and when we break loose we find ourselves on the pier at Brighton or heroically scaling Beachy Head. We pass our dreams of adventure on to hopeful and undazzled youth, browsing greedily in the breathless pages of Prescott. We are not even sure that we want to go now, so habituated have we become to the familiar tread-mill. I daresay the Carisbrooke donkey would have been broken-hearted at the idea of a trip to

Dream Journeys

Cowes. We are like Johnson when he was asked if he would not like to see Giant's Causeway. "Sir, I should like to see it, but I should not like *to go to see it.*"

It would be pleasant if we could educate our dreams to spirit us away without all the trouble of tickets and luggage and travel to the sights and experiences we have missed. Do not tell me it would be an idle illusion. There was no illusion in my island. I can see it in my mind as clearly as any place I ever visited in the flesh, and if I had the skill I could draw its hills and paint its tranquil sea and sunny sands for you. To-night I hope to spend with Mummery in the Alps.

ON COMING HOME

A FRIEND of mine found himself the other day on the platform of a country station in the south of Scotland near the sea-coast. A middle-aged couple were the only people visible, and they sat together on the single form provided for waiting passengers. They did not speak, but just sat and gazed at the rails, at the opposite platform, at the fields beyond, at the clouds above, at anything, in fact, within the range of vision. My friend went and sat beside them to wait for his train. Presently another person, a woman, appeared, and advancing to the other two, addressed them. She wondered what train the couple were waiting for. Was their holiday over?

"Oh no," said the woman. "We've another week yet."

"Then maybe ye're waiting for a friend?" speired the other.

"No," replied the woman. "We're juist sitting. We like to come here in the evening and see the trains come in and out. It's a change, and it makes us think of home. Eh," she said, with a sudden fervour that spoke of inward agonies, "you do miss your home comforts on a holiday."

I fancy this excellent woman, sitting on the platform to watch the trains go homewards, and yearning for the day to come when she will take a seat in one of them, disclosed a secret which many of us share, but few of us have the courage to confess. She was bored by her holiday. It was her annual Purgatory, her time of exile by the alien waters of Babylon.

16

On Coming Home

There she sat while the commonplaces of her home life, her comfortable bed, the mysteries of her larder, the gossip of her neighbours, the dusting of the front parlour, the trials of shopping, her good man's going and returning, the mending of the children's stockings, and all the little somethings-and-nothings that made up her daily round, assumed a glamour and a pathos that familiarity had deadened. She had to go away from home to discover it again. She had to get out of her rut in order to find that she could not be happy anywhere else. Then she could say with Touchstone, "So this is the forest of Arden: well, when I was at home I was in a better place."

It does not follow that her holiday was a failure. It was a most successful holiday. The main purpose of a holiday is to make us home-sick. We go to the forest of Arden in order that we may be reconciled to No. 14, Beulah Avenue, Peckham. We sit and throw stones on the beach in the sunshine until we get sick of doing nothing in particular, and dream of the 8.32 from Tooting as the children of Israel dreamed of the fat pastures of Canaan. We climb the Jungfrau and explore the solitudes of the glaciers so that we can recover the rapture of Clapham Common and the felicities of Hampstead Heath. We endure the dreary formalities of hotel life and the petty larcenies of the boarding-house in order that we may enjoy with renewed zest the ease and liberties of our own fireside.

In short, we go on a holiday for the pleasure of coming back. The humiliating truth is, of course, providentially concealed from us. If it were not, we

On Coming Home

should stay at home and never see it afresh through the pleasant medium of distance and separation. But no experience of past disillusions dims the glow of the holiday emotion. I have no doubt that the couple on the platform set out from Auld Reekie with the delight of children let out from school. We all know the feeling. "Behold . . . Beyond . . ." cried young Ruskin when the distant vision of the snowy battlements of the Oberland first burst on his astonished eyes. "Behold . . . Beyond," we cry as we pile up the luggage and start on the happy pilgrimage. And the emotion is worth having, even though we know it will end in a sigh of relief when we reach No. 14, Beulah Avenue again and sink into the familiar arm-chair and mow the bit of lawn that has grown shaggy in our absence, and exchange reminiscences with No. 13 over the fence, and feel the pleasant web of habit enveloping us once more.

It is when the holiday is over that we begin to enjoy it. Then we come, as Gissing says, under the law that wills that the day must die before we can enjoy to the full its light and odour. We are never, by the perversity of our nature, quite so happy as we think we were after the event had become a memory, and no doubt by next spring the couple who sat on the station platform watching the homeward-bound trains with longing eyes will recall the gay holiday they had without a suspicion that they welcomed the end of it as children welcome release from school. The illusion will only mean that they are a little sick of home again, and that they need the violent medicine of a holiday to make them home-sick once more.

A LOG FIRE

I CAME in from the woods with a settled purpose. I would spend the evening in exalting the beauty of these wonderful November days in the country. The idea presented itself to me not merely as a pleasure but as a duty. Long enough had November been misjudged and slandered, usually by Cockney poets like Tom Hood, who looked at it through the fogs of a million coal fires. Bare justice demanded that the truth should out, that the world should be told of this beautiful though aged spinster of the months who clothed the landscape in such a radiant garment of sunshine, carpeted the beech-woods with such a glow of gold and russet, filled the hedgerows with the scarlet of the hips and haws, the wine-red of the blackthorn, and the yellow of the guelder rose, and awoke the thrushes from their late summer silence.

This fervour for my Lady November is no new passion. There are certain things about which I have never made up my mind, and about which, I suppose, I never shall make up my mind. That is to say I make it up, and then unmake it, after which I remake it, like the child on the sea-shore who sees his sand-castle swept away by one tide, and returns to build it for another tide to sweep away. Thus, if I say that I prefer Bach's Concerto for Two Violins to any piece of music I have ever heard, I do not guarantee that a year hence I may not be found swearing by the Londonderry air, or a Hebridean song (the *Island*

A Log Fire

Shieling Song, for example), or the *Magic Flute*, or something from Schumann. A year later I may be round to the intertwined loveliness of the two violins again. And if I affirm that the *Brothers Karamazov* is the greatest achievement of the imagination since Shakespeare, I do not promise not to say the same thing of something else, *David Copperfield* or *Les Misérables*, when, after a due interval, I express my view again. And so with pictures and authors and towns and trees and flowers—in short, all the things that appeal to the changing emotions or to that vague and unstable thing called taste.

So it is in regard to the merits of the months. I have been trying all my life to come to a final decision on this great question. It seems absurd that one should spend, as I have spent, fifty or sixty years doing little else but sample the months without arriving at a fixed and irrevocable conclusion as to which I like best. But that is the case. I am a mere Don Juan with the months. I go flirting about from one to the other, swearing that each is more beautiful than her rivals. When I am with June it seems absurd that there should be anything else than June, and when I am with August I would not sacrifice August with its waving cornfields and its sound of the reaper for half the calendar. But then comes September, and I chant Swinburne to her as though I had never loved another:

> September! all glorious with gold as a king
>   In the raiment of triumph attired,
> Outlightening the summer, outsweetening the spring,
> It broods o'er the woodlands with limitless wing,
>   A presence of all men desired.

A Log Fire

I do not doubt that I have declared that October, ruddy October, chill October, is the pick of the bunch, and I know that on the first bright day in February, when I see the snowdrops peeping out and hear the rooks in the elms, I shall be found declaring that this is the choicest moment of the year. And April—April with the trees bursting into green and the meadows "smo'ered wi' new grass," as they say in the dales, and the birds coming up from the south bringing tidings of the summer—well, what can one say of April, Shakespeare's April, Shakespeare's "sweet o' the year," except that there is none like her?

But I know that when May comes in and the orchards burst into foam, and the lilac, laburnum and pink hawthorn make every suburban street lyrical with colour and the beech-woods are clothed in that first tender green that seems to make the sunlight sing as it streams through and dapples the golden carpet of last year's leaves with light and shade, and the bees are humming like an orchestra in the cherry and damson trees and the birds are singing as though they are divinely drunk, and the first brood of young swallows are making their trial flights from the nest in the barn and

> When nothing that asks for bliss
> Asking aright is denied,
> And half of the world a bridegroom is
> And half the world a bride.

—then I know that I shall desert even My Lady April and give the palm to the undespoiled

A Log Fire

splendour of May, singing meanwhile with Francis Thompson:

> By Goddés fay, by Goddés fay,
>   It is the month, the merry month,
> It is the merry month of May.

In this shameless wandering of the affections I have come round once more to November, and I marvel, as I have marvelled many a year before, that the poets have left unsung the elderly beauties of this month, the quietude of its tones, the sombre dignity of its landscape, the sense of a noble passing, the fading colours, the falling leaves, the winds changing to a note of requiem among the dismantled branches—

> Bare ruined choirs where late the sweet birds sang.

And lamenting this neglect I resolved to pay my tribute. But first I must make up the fire, for though my Lady November is beautiful she is austere. She has frozen the pump and the grass is thick with hoarfrost, and to be just to her one must be warm. So I piled on the logs and prepared to be warm and enthusiastic.

Then I did a foolish thing, I sat down in an armchair and surrendered myself to the fire's comfortable companionship. There is nothing more friendly or talkative than a fire. Even a coal fire, if you look at it steadfastly, will become as communicative as a maiden aunt. It knows all the gossip of the family, especially the gossip about old, forgotten things. It will talk to you of events so remote that they seem to belong to the country of dreams. It will bring out faded portraits, and sing old songs, and burst into

A Log Fire

laughter that you have not heard perhaps for forty years, and revive antique jokes, and hand round steaming elderberry wine o' Christmas nights, and make shadowgraphs on the wall as if you were a little boy again, and send you sliding and skating under the glittering stars. It forgets nothing about you, and it tells its memories so cheerfully and serenely that it leaves nothing for tears. All this, even a coal-fire will do when it is really in the vein and you have time to sit and listen.

But a wood fire has a magic beyond this. Its very smell is an intoxication as rapturous as romance, compounded of all you have read of the backwoods, of memories of the charcoal-burners, and of Coal Munk Peter, of tales of the woodlands, Tristan and Iseult, and Robin Hood, and Good King Wenceslaus, and the Children of the New Forest, of Giles Winterbourne and Marty South, and all the delightful people with whom the mind loves to go a-gypsying far away from this foolish world. Of course, you have to be something of a sentimentalist or a romantic to feel all this—such a person as I once walked with for a month in the Black Forest, to whom the smell of the woodlands was as exciting as wine, and the sight of a charcoal-burner's camp a sort of apocalyptic vision. How well I remember those summer nights when, leaving the forest inn, we would plunge into the woodlands, he singing that haunting air *Der Mai ist gekommen* and interrupting it with a shout as he saw the glimmer of the charcoal-burner's fire through the boles of the pine trees. . . .

But a wood fire is not only an idyll. It is an occupa-

A Log Fire

tion. With a coal fire it is different. You put on a shovel of coals, and there's an end of it. But a wood fire will furnish light and pleasing employment for a whole evening. And by a wood fire I do not mean those splinters of wood that you buy in towns, but thumping logs—beech or apple or fir, as the case may be—a yard or two long and with the bark intact that you lay across the fire-dogs and turn round and round until they are burned through at the centre and fall into the embers beneath in a glorious blaze, sending out such a generous warmth as only comes from a wood fire. Once or twice I drew myself away from this seductive task and sat down at the table, determined to write such a moving panegyric on November as would make it the haughtiest month of the year. Once I even went outside to get inspiration from the stars and the moon that was flooding the valley with a mystic light and the hoar-frost that lay like a white garment over the orchard. I heard the hoot of the owl in the copse near by and the sound of the wind in the trees and the barking of a distant dog and came back to my task with a stern resolve to see it through. But the struggle was in vain. Always there was some nice readjustment of the logs necessary to call me to the charmed circle of the wood fire; always at the end I found myself planted in the arm-chair watching the changing scenery of the glowing embers.

So the article was not written after all. Perhaps it was as well, for I do not think I have the brush to do justice to My Lady November. It may be that that is why the wood fire had so easy a triumph.

ON SAYING "PLEASE"

THE young lift-man in a City office who threw a passenger out of his lift the other morning and was fined for the offence was undoubtedly in the wrong. It was a question of "Please." The complainant, entering the lift, said, "Top." The lift-man demanded, "Top—please," and this concession being refused he not only declined to comply with the instruction, but hurled the passenger out of the lift. This, of course, was carrying a comment on manners too far. Discourtesy is not a legal offence, and it does not excuse assault and battery. If a burglar breaks into my house and I knock him down the law will acquit me, and if I am physically assaulted it will permit me to retaliate with reasonable violence. It does this because the burglar and my assailant have broken quite definite commands of the law. But no legal system could attempt to legislate against bad manners, or could sanction the use of violence against something which it does not itself recognise as a legally punishable offence. And whatever our sympathy with the lift-man, we must admit that the law is reasonable. It would never do if we were at liberty to box people's ears because we did not like their behaviour, or the tone of their voices, or the scowl on their faces. Our fists would never be idle, and the gutters of the City would run with blood all day.

On Saying " Please "

I may be as uncivil as I please and the law will protect me against violent retaliation. I may be haughty or boorish and there is no penalty to pay except the penalty of being written down an ill-mannered fellow. The law does not compel me to say "Please" or to attune my voice to other people's sensibilities any more than it says that I shall not wax my moustache or dye my hair or wear ringlets down my back. It does not recognise the laceration of our feelings as a case for compensation. There is no allowance for moral and intellectual damages in these matters.

This does not mean that the damages are negligible. It is probable that the lift-man was much more acutely hurt by what he regarded as a slur upon his social standing than he would have been if he had had a kick on the shins, for which he could have got legal redress. The pain of a kick on the shins soon passes away, but the pain of a wound to our self-respect or our vanity may poison a whole day. I can imagine that lift-man, denied the relief of throwing the author of his wound out of the lift, brooding over the insult by the hour, and visiting it on his wife in the evening as the only way of restoring his equilibrium. For there are few things more catching than bad temper and bad manners. When Sir Anthony Absolute bullied Captain Absolute, the latter went out and bullied his man Fag, whereupon Fag went downstairs and kicked the page-boy. Probably the man who said "Top" to the lift-man was really only getting back on his employer who had not said "Good morning" to him because he himself had been

On Saying " Please "

hen-pecked at breakfast by his wife, to whom the cook had been insolent because the housemaid had "answered her back." We infect the world with our ill-humours. Bad manners probably do more to poison the stream of the general life than all the crimes in the calendar. For one wife who gets a black eye from an otherwise good-natured husband there are a hundred who live a life of martyrdom under the shadow of a morose temper. But all the same the law cannot become the guardian of our private manners. No Decalogue could cover the vast area of offences and no court could administer a law which governed our social civilities, our speech, the tilt of our eye-brows and all our moods and manners.

But though we are bound to endorse the verdict against the lift-man, most people will have a certain sympathy with him. While it is true that there is no law that compels us to say "Please," there is a social practice much older and more sacred than any law which enjoins us to be civil. And the first require-ment of civility is that we should acknowledge a service. "Please" and "Thank you" are the small change with which we pay our way as social beings. They are the little courtesies by which we keep the machine of life oiled and running sweetly. They put our intercourse upon the basis of a friendly co-opera-tion, an easy give-and-take, instead of on the basis of superiors dictating to inferiors. It is a very vulgar mind that would wish to command where he can have the service for asking, and have it with willing-ness and good-feeling instead of resentment.

I should like to "feature" in this connection my

On Saying " Please "

friend the polite conductor. By this discriminating title I do not intend to suggest a rebuke to conductors generally. On the contrary, I am disposed to think that there are few classes of men who come through the ordeal of a very trying calling better than bus conductors do. Here and there you will meet an unpleasant specimen who regards the passengers as his natural enemies—as creatures whose chief purpose on the bus is to cheat him, and who can only be kept reasonably honest by a loud voice and an aggressive manner. But this type is rare— rarer than it used to be. I fancy the public owes much to the Underground Railway Company, which also runs the buses, for insisting on a certain standard of civility in its servants, and taking care that that standard is observed. In doing this it not only makes things pleasant for the travelling public, but performs an important social service.

It is not, therefore, with any feeling of unfriendliness to conductors as a class that I pay a tribute to a particular member of that class. I first became conscious of his existence one day when I jumped on to a bus and found that I had left home without any money in my pocket. Everyone has had the experience and knows the feeling, the mixed feeling, which the discovery arouses. You are annoyed because you look like a fool at the best, and like a knave at the worst. You would not be at all surprised if the conductor eyed you coldly as much as to say, "Yes, I know that stale old trick. Now then, off you get." And even if the conductor is a good fellow and lets you down easily, you are faced with the necessity of going back, and the inconvenience, perhaps, of missing your train or your engagement.

Having searched my pockets in vain for stray coppers, and having found I was utterly penniless, I told the conductor with as honest a face as I could assume that I couldn't pay the fare, and must go back for money. "Oh, you needn't get off: that's all right," said he. "All right," said I, "but I haven't a copper on me." "Oh, I'll book you through," he replied. "Where d'ye want to go?" and he handled his bundle of tickets with the air of a man who was prepared to give me a ticket for anywhere from the Bank to Hong Kong. I said it was very kind of him, and told him where I wanted to go, and as he gave me the ticket I said, "But where shall I send the fare?" "Oh, you'll see me some day all right," he said cheerfully, as he turned to go. And then, luckily, my fingers, still wandering in the corners of my pockets, lighted on a shilling, and the account was squared. But that fact did not lessen the glow of pleasure which so good-natured an action had given me.

A few days after my most sensitive toe was trampled on rather heavily as I sat reading on the top of a bus. I looked up with some anger and more agony, and saw my friend of the cheerful countenance. "Sorry, sir," he said. "I know these are heavy boots. Got 'em because my own feet get trod on so much, and now I'm treading on other people's. Hope I didn't hurt you, sir." He had hurt me but he was so nice about it that I assured him he hadn't. After this I began to observe him whenever I boarded his bus, and found a curious pleasure in the constant good-nature of his bearing. He seemed to have an inexhaustible fund of patience and a gift for making his passengers comfortable. I noticed that if it was raining he would run up the stairs to give someone the tip that there was "room inside." With old people he was as considerate as a son, and with children as solicitous as a father. He had evidently a peculiarly warm place in his heart for young people, and always indulged in some merry jest with them. If he had a blind man on board it was not enough to set him down safely on the pavement. He would call to Bill in front to wait while he took him across the road or round the corner, or otherwise safely on his way. In short, I found that he irradiated such an atmosphere of good-temper and kindliness that a journey with him was a lesson in natural courtesy and good manners.

What struck me particularly was the ease with which he got through his work. If bad manners are infectious, so also are good manners. If we encounter incivility most of us are apt to become uncivil, but it is an unusually uncouth person who can be disagreeable with sunny people. It is with manners as with the weather. "Nothing clears up my spirits like a fine day," said Keats, and a cheerful person descends on even the gloomiest of us with something of the benediction of a fine day. And so it was always fine weather on the polite conductor's bus, and his own civility, his conciliatory address and good-humoured bearing, infected his passengers. In lightening their spirits he lightened his own task. His gaiety was not a wasteful luxury, but a sound investment.

I have missed him from my bus route of late; but

On Saying " Please "

I hope that only means that he has carried his sunshine on to another road. It cannot be too widely
diffused in a rather drab world. And I make no
apologies for writing a panegyric on an unknown
bus conductor. If Wordsworth could gather lessons
of wisdom from the poor leech-gatherer "on the
lonely moor," I see no reason why lesser people
should not take lessons in conduct from one who
shows how a very modest calling may be dignified by
good-temper and kindly feeling.

It is a matter of general agreement that the war
has had a chilling effect upon those little every-day
civilities of behaviour that sweeten the general air.
We must get those civilities back if we are to make
life kindly and tolerable for each other. We cannot
get them back by invoking the law. The policeman
is a necessary symbol and the law is a necessary institution for a society that is still somewhat lower
than the angels. But the law can only protect us
against material attack. Nor will the lift-man's way
of meeting moral affront by physical violence help
us to restore the civilities. I suggest to him that he
would have had a more subtle and effective revenge
if he had treated the gentleman who would not say
"Please" with elaborate politeness. He would have
had the victory, not only over the boor, but over himself, and that is the victory that counts. The polite
man may lose the material advantage, but he always
has the spiritual victory. I commend to the lift-man
a story of Chesterfield. In his time the London streets
were without the pavements of to-day, and the man
who "took the wall" had the driest footing. "I never

give the wall to a scoundrel," said a man who met
Chesterfield one day in the street. "I always do,"
said Chesterfield, stepping with a bow into the road.
I hope the lift-man will agree that his revenge was
much more sweet than if he had flung the fellow
into the mud.

BILLITCH AT LORD'S

OF course, there were others there besides Bill. There were twenty thousand people there. There was the whole Oval crowd there. I was there—I always try to put in a day at Lord's when the Oval crowd charges across the river with its jolly plebeian war-cries and swarms into the enclosure at St. John's Wood like a crowd of happy children. It makes me feel young again to be caught in that tide of fresh enthusiasm. I know that is how I used to feel in the good old days of the 'eighties when I used to set out with my lunch to the Oval to see Walter Read and Lohmann and K. J. Key and M. P. Bowden and Abel and Lockwood and Tom Richardson and all the glorious company who filled the stage then. What heroes they were! What scenes we saw! What bowling, what batting, what fielding! I daresay the heroes of to-day are as heroic as those of whom I speak; but not for me.

Cricket, to the ageing mind, is never what it used to be; it is always looking back to some golden age when it flourished, like chivalry, in a pure and unsullied world. My father used to talk to me with fervour about the heroic deeds of Caffyn and Julius Cæsar, and I talk to young people about the incomparable skill of Grace and Steel and Lohmann, and they no doubt will be eloquent to their children about

Billitch at Lord's

Hobbs and Gregory. And so on. Francis Thompson explained the secret of the golden age when he sang:

Oh, my Hornby and my Barlow *long ago*.

That is it. It is that "long ago" that makes our giants so gigantesque. Cricketers, as the old gentleman said of the peaches, are not so fine as they were in our young days. How could they be? Why have we lived all these years if we are not allowed to have seen greater things than these youngsters who are shouldering us out of the way have ever seen? Of course, they don't believe in "our Hornbys and our Barlows long ago" any more than I believed when a boy that Caffyn and Julius Cæsar could hold a candle to W. G. or Walter Read, and they will find that their children will think lightly of Hobbs in comparison with some contemporary god of their idolatry.

But whatever change has taken place in cricket— or in me—I swear there is no change in the jolly Oval crowd. It is, as it has always been, the liveliest, most intense, most good-humoured mob that ever shouted itself hoarse at cricket. It is as different from the Lord's crowd as a country fair is from the Church Congress. At Lord's we take our cricket as solemnly as if we were at a prayer-meeting. We sit and smoke and knit our brows with portentous gravity. Sometimes we forget ourselves and say: "Well run, sir!" or "Missed. By Jove!" Then we turn round to see if anybody has heard us. We have even been known to clap; but these extravagances are rare. Generally we end by falling asleep.

But we were done out of our sleep on Monday.

Billitch at Lord's

There's no possibility of sleep when the Oval crowd is about and when they have brought Billitch with them. At Lord's we never have a popular hero or a comic figure. Cricket is far too serious a thing to turn to fun. If Little Tich came and played at Lord's, we should not smile. We should take him very seriously, and call him Mr. William Tich if he came out of the front-door of the pavilion, and Tich (W.) if he came out of the side-door. On Monday we had several bad shocks to our sense of the solemnities of cricket. For example, we saw Fender, the Surrey captain, lead the "gentlemen" members of his team to the professionals' quarters and bring his team out to the field in a body, just for all the world as though they were all one flesh and blood. It was a painful sight, and many of us closed our eyes rather than look upon it. We felt that Bolshevism had invaded our sanctuary at last.

And then there was that unseemly enthusiasm for Billitch. I don't know what there is about Bill that makes him such an idol of the Oval crowd; but there it is. If Bill went on to bowl the ring shouted, "Good ole Bill"; if he went off bowling it said that, "Ole Bill wants a rest"; if he hit a ball it said, "That's one for ole Bill"; if he missed a ball it said, "Ole Bill let that go by"; if he tapped the wicket with his bat it was confident that "Ole Bill had found a narsty spot"; if he made a short run it shouted, "Brayvo, ole Bill." I think that if he had stopped to blow his nose the crowd would have blown its nose too, for the pleasure of keeping him company.

It is not that Billitch is a comic figure, as Johnny

Billitch at Lord's

Briggs used to be. Nor an incomparable cricketer, as Lohmann used to be. Nor of home product from Mitcham Common, for I think he comes from Lancashire. But he has a certain liveliness, a sense of enjoying everything he does, and putting his whole heart into it, that gives a lusty spirit to the game and touches the affections of the Oval crowd, which always mixes up its affections with its cricket. And his name does the rest. It is an irresistible name. You can go on saying Billitch all day without growing weary. It will suit any circumstances and go to any rhythm. What jolly verses old Craig would weave about it if he could come back and hawk poems to us on sunny afternoons. But it needed the Oval crowd to discover the riches of that name. If Billitch had come to Lord's he would not have been Billitch at all. He would have been Hitch (W.) and as solemn as all the rest of us. I wish we were as merry at Lord's as they are at the Oval.

ON SHOP WINDOWS

IT is one of the consolations of being unemployed that one has time to look in the shop windows. When I was among the employed I never looked in shop windows. I was shot like a shuttle in a loom from home to office and from engagement to engagement, and had no time to saunter along and "stand and stare." It was not merely that I had no time for shop windows: I thought I had no taste for shop windows. If I walked down Regent Street with Jane I was sensible of a certain impatience when she made a sudden left-wheel and stood transfixed before some brilliant idea of the window-dresser. I declined to wheel to the left. I stood implacably in the middle of the pavement, looking severely ahead or around or above. I wanted to be getting on with the war. I was a serious person, with a soul above the frivolities of shop windows. No doubt there was something of a pose in this behaviour. There is usually something of a pose in us when we feel superior.

But with the inheritance of leisure I have become more humble-minded. I not only wheel to the left when Jane wheels, but I wheel to the left on my own account. I am becoming a student of shop windows. I find them as interesting as a hedgerow in the country. I can tell you the price of things. I

On Shop Windows

can discuss with you the relative merits of Marshall
and Snelgrove and Peter Robinson, and the name of
Mr. Selfridge falls trippingly from my tongue. There
is not a tailor's shop between the Law Courts and
Marble Arch that I have not peered into, and if you
want to know where a good line in boots is to be had
or where motor-cars are cheap to-day or precious
stones should be sought I am worth consulting. No
longer does Jane regard a walk down Regent Street
with me as an affliction. I am a companion after her
own heart—if not an expert, at least an intelligent
amateur. A touch on my arm, and I wheel to the left
with military precision and line up in front of the
window and discuss the contents in no unenlightened
spirit. My opinion is regarded. I am asked questions.
I am listened to with respect. My taste in hats is
becoming a proverb, and it is allowed that I have
a good eye for colour.

In this new-found diversion I am catholic in my
tastes. You may see me lost in thought before a
furniture shop or a fruit shop, or examining trom-
bones or Kodaks, or looking at old colour prints or
old books, or studying old china, or simply standing
amused among a crowd of other idlers watching the
kittens at play in the naturalist's shop window. There
is no covetousness in all this. I am conscious of no
yearnings for unattainable things. On the contrary,
I am astonished at the number of things I can
do without.

Nor am I tempted to go inside the shops.

May day seldom looks
Up in the country as it does in books.

On Shop Windows

And I know that shop windows are no more like the inside of shops than a company prospectus is like the company's balance-sheet. You see, let us say, a pair of shoes in the window at twenty-five shillings. It would be a crime to let that pair of shoes go, you say. It is what you have been looking for—something "good-cheap," as the old English phrase went. You go inside and allude falteringly to that cheap line in the window. The salesman observes the falter. He speaks coldly of that attractive-looking bait. You feebly insist, and he tries it on, making you sensible the while that a person like you would be dishonoured by such footwear, that he is surprised you should think that a person of your obvious quality can appear abroad in such inferior leathers. Moreover, aren't they a leetle tight across the instep? And unfortunately he hasn't the next size in stock. . . . Now here is a perfect shoe, best box-calf, soft as kid, durable as brass, last a lifetime. . . . The price? The fellow looks inside as though the question of price had not occurred to him, as though it had no relation to the subject. . . . Fifty-five shillings. And as you leave the shop worsted, wearing the shoes, you fancy you hear a slight chuckle of derision from the victor.

There are, of course, people who love shopping and whose life is irradiated by victories at the counter. They are chiefly women, but I have known men who had gifts in this line of no mean order. They could march into a shop as boldly as any woman and have the place turned upside down and go away without spending a copper, carrying their heads as high and

On Shop Windows

haughtily as you please. But men of this heroic mould are rare. Men are usually much too mean-spirited, too humble, too timid to be fit to go into a shop to buy anything. Perhaps I ought to say they are too proud. They would slink out, if they could do so unobserved. They would decline to buy what they don't want to buy if their vanity would permit them. But they cannot face the ordeal. They cannot leave the impression that they are not rolling in riches and are not able to buy anything in the shop, whether they want it or not. And it is only fair to us to say that sometimes we fall from compassion. We buy because the lady has been so attentive—or has such an agreeable presence—that we have not the courage to disappoint her or, less creditably, to lose her favourable opinion.

Now women, of course, are afflicted with none of these handicaps. The trouble with men as shoppers is that they are incurable amateurs and sentimentalists. They not only do not know the ropes; they do not know that there are any ropes to know. They are just babes and sucklings at the business. You can see the Delilah behind the counter smiling pityingly and even contemptuously to herself as they approach with their mouths wide open to receive the hook. She chooses her bait under the poor simpletons' noses, and lands them without a struggle. She knows that they will take any old thing at any old price. But a woman marches to the attack as the soldier marches to battle. She is for the rigour of the game. The shop is her battlefield, and she surveys it with the eye of the professional warrior. And Delilah

On Shop Windows

prepares to receive her as an enemy worthy of her steel. All her faculties are aroused, all her suspicions are awakened. She expects no quarter, and she will give none.

Here is Pamela, for example, accompanied by Roderick, halting rather shamefacedly in the rear. Roderick has never seen Pamela on the warpath before, and it is a terrifying revelation. He had thought she was so kind-hearted and genial that everybody must love her, but he grows crimson as he sees the progress of the duel. This is not the Pamela he knew: this is a very Amazon of a woman, armed to the teeth, clothed in an icy disapproval of everything, riding down her foe with Prussian frightfulness. And all over a matter of a handbag. The counter is piled with handbags, and Pamela examines each with relentless thoroughness and increasing dissatisfaction. She must have more handbags. And Delilah with darkening brows ransacks the store for the last handbag. She understands the game, but she is helpless, and when at the end of the battle Pamela coldly remarks that they are not what she wants, and that she will just take one of those tops, Delilah knows that she has been defeated. "I only wanted a top, you see," says Pamela to Roderick sweetly as they leave the shop, "but I wanted to see how the bags were fitted to them."

Or to understand the gulf that separates men and women in the art and science of shopping, see my Lady Bareacres at the mantlemaker's, accompanied by a lady companion. All the riches of the establishment are displayed before her, and she parades in

On Shop Windows

front of the mirror in an endless succession of flowing robes. She gives the impression of inexhaustible good intentions, but she finds that there is nothing that suits her, and she goes away to repeat the performance elsewhere. And as she goes Delilah looks daggers at the companion who has come with her ladyship to get hints for the garment that she is to make for her.

The man has not been born who could play so high a hand as that. Whether his inferiority in the great art of shopping is to be accounted to him as a virtue or a shame may be left to the moralists to discuss; but the fact is indisputable enough. He knows his weakness, and rarely goes into a shop except in the last extremity or under the competent guardianship of a woman. He can look in shop windows if he have firmness of mind and can say, "Danton, no weakness!" with the assurance that Danton will not bolt inside. But there is one sort of shop window before which the least of us are safe. And it transcends all shop windows in interest. It is the window through which you look into the far places of the earth. Canada and Queensland, British Columbia and New Zealand. The Strand is lit up with glimpses of these distant horizons—landscapes waving with corn, landscapes flowing with milk and honey, bales of fleecy wool, sugar-canes like scaffold poles, peaches that make the mouth water, pumpkins as large as the full moon, prodigious trout that would make the angler's heart sing, snow mountains and climbing-boots, a thousand invitations to come out into the wide spaces of the earth, where plenty and freedom and the sunshine await you. I daresay it is an illusion. I daresay the

On Shop Windows

wide spaces of the earth are very unlike these wonderful windows. But I love to look in them and to feel that they are true. They almost make me wish that I were young again—young enough to set out

> For to admire and for to see,
> For to behold the world so wide.

A DAY WITH THE BEES

THERE is a prevalent notion that the country is a good place to work in. The quiet of the country, so runs the theory, leaves the mind undistracted, calm and able to concentrate on the task in hand. It is a plausible theory, but it is untrue. In town the movement, noise and ceaseless unrest form a welter of sound that has no more personal significance than the lapping of the waves on the sea-shore. It does not disturb—it rather composes the mind. It is the irrelevant babble of the world, enormous but signifying nothing, in the midst of which the mind is at ease and self-contained. But in the country every sound has an individual meaning that breaks in upon the quiet and demands attention. It is not general; it is particular. Take to-day, for example. I had sat down after breakfast, determined to traverse the Sahara on which I am engaged and to reach the oasis of a chapter-ending by nightfall.

But I had hardly begun when a bumble bee flew in at the open door on one side of the room and made for the closed window on the other side. The buzz of a bumble bee in the open air makes a substantial volume of sound. But inside the room this turbulent fellow sounded like an aeroplane as he roared against the window-panes in his frantic efforts to get through. Give him time, I thought. He will discover that there

A Day with the Bees

is no thoroughfare by the window and will return by the way he came in. Let me get on with my work. But the bumble bee has as little sense in the matter of exits and entrances as the wasp has, and my visitor kept up such a thunder against the window-panes that I was compelled to surrender, got up, opened the window, and with a judicious thrust with a newspaper piloted the fellow out into the open air.

It was a bad beginning for the journey across the Sahara; but I sat down, composed myself afresh, and started again, ignoring the thrush who was calling his hardest to me just outside the window to come out and see what a glorious sunshiny day we had got at last. But I was hardly launched again on my journey when I became conscious of unusual sounds in the garden. I looked out and saw the odd man, who had been banking up the potatoes, shielding himself as if from a storm and uttering strange cries. I left the desert again and rushed out. Everybody else in the house I found was rushing out. There, swirling like a cloud of dust across the garden, was a swarm of bees which had swept down from the hills and across the meadow land behind us and were evidently on the point of settling. They passed by the house with the boom of ten thousand wings and came to rest in a hawthorn bush on the road below. It was no business of mine. The expert was out with veil and gloves on for the fray and could very well manage without my help; but no amount of familiarity makes me able to resist the call of a swarm of bees, and I forgot all about Sahara until we returned

A Day with the Bees

triumphantly with a branch bearing a vast coagulated mass of bees and succeeded in housing them in a spare hive.

Then I remembered Sahara and, like Mr. Snodgrass (the exercise having warmed me unduly), I took off my coat and announced to myself that "Now I am about to begin." A ring at the telephone bell! A swarm of bees had settled on the roof of a house a mile or two away, and would we be so kind as to take them away. Off went the expert as fast as petrol could carry her, and I returned to my lonely plough and the desert sands. But this day was doomed for me by the warm sun that had set all the surplus population of the hives for miles round trekking to new quarters. The cold Spring and the wet May and early June had kept the bee world quiescent. Looking in the hives we could see all the preparations for swarming in progress, but the weather had been unpropitious and now with this sudden burst of summer all the tide of repressed life was released, and it seemed that the whole countryside was alive with bees in flight from their crowded homes to new lodgings. Before the expert returned there was sensation once more in the garden. No. 5 had swarmed, and down between the spruce-trees and the hedge the air was thick with the migrants. Usually our swarms settle in the hedge while the couriers fly far and wide to reconnoitre for suitable quarters. And it is in this interval of waiting that they are hived afresh. But this swarm neither settled in the hedge nor flew away with that sudden inspiration which sometimes seizes them. They swirled round and round

A Day with the Bees

like a tornado that had lost its way. Then they were observed to be returning to the hive they had left.

Here was a mystery indeed. Had the queen changed her mind and gone back, or had she by some miracle eluded her enormous family? The arrival of the expert, with her new capture, relieved us of responsibility in the matter. She opened the hive and took out the frames on which the bees were massed, but the queen, discoverable by her larger size, was not to be seen. At last, outside on the path, we saw a group of bees and in the midst of them the queen. The adventure had been too much for her powers, or perhaps she had defective wings. She was put back in the hive, and what the workers thought about the flight that failed I shall never know. But a new home to which the queen had no need to fly was soon at their disposal.

By this time the day was far advanced, but my journey across Sahara had hardly begun, and even now the interruptions from the bees were not at an end. For the third time there was commotion in the garden; on this occasion the note was tragedy. One of the hens, which had had some accident, was confined in a coop as a sort of convalescent home. Its water-supply was outside and thither the bees had gone to drink. One of them, objecting to the beak that came out of the coop, stung the hen near the eye, and the smell of the acid infuriated its fellows and soon the unhappy hen was enveloped in a cloud of bees each stabbing it in its vulnerable spot. When its plight was discovered the poor creature was insensible and apparently dying. With difficulty the assailants

A Day with the Bees

were driven off and the victim was put out of its misery.

When night came I was still ploughing my lonely furrow with no hope of reaching the goal for which I had started out so hopefully in the morning. No, the country is too exciting a place to work in. Give me the solitude of London, where there are no bees to swarm and no thrushes to keep telling one what a fine day it is in the garden.

ON SHAKING HANDS

IF there is one custom that might be assumed to be beyond criticism it is the custom of shaking hands; but it seems that even this innocent and amiable practice is upon its trial. A heavy indictment has been directed against it in the Press on hygienic grounds, and we are urged to adopt some more healthy mode of expressing our mutual emotion when we meet or part. I think it would need a pretty stiff Act of Parliament and a heavy code of penalties to break us of so ingrained a habit. Of course, there are many people in the world who go through life without ever shaking hands. Probably most people in the world manage to do so. The Japanese bows, and the Indian salaams, and the Chinese makes a grave motion of the hand, and the Arab touches the breast of his friend at parting with the tips of his fingers.

By comparison with these modes of salutation it may be that our Western custom of shaking each other by the hand seems coarse and bucolic, just as our custom of promiscuous kissing seems an unintelligible indecency to the Japanese, to whom osculation has an exclusive sexual significance that we do not attach to it. In the matter of kissing, it is true, we have become much more restrained than our ancestors. Everyone has read the famous passage in Erasmus' letters in which he describes how people

On Shaking Hands

used to kiss in Tudor England, and how, by the way, that learned and holy man enjoyed it. He could not write so of us to-day. And there is one connection in which kissing has never been a common form of salutation with us. Masculine kissing is an entirely Continental habit, chiefly cultivated among the Russians. The greatest display of kissing I have ever witnessed was at Prince Kropotkin's house—he was then living at Brighton—on his seventieth birthday. A procession of aged and bearded Russian patriarchs came to bring greetings, and as each one entered the room he rushed at the sage, flung his arms about his neck, and gave him a resounding smack on each whiskered cheek, and Kropotkin gave resounding smacks in return.

This is carrying heartiness too far for our austerer tastes. I do not think that Englishmen could be bribed to kiss each other, but I cannot conceive that they will ever be argued out of shaking hands with each other. A greeting which we really feel without a grip of the hand to accompany it would seem like a repulse, or a sacrilege. It would be a bond without the seal—as cold as a stepmother's breath, as official as a typewritten letter with a typewritten signature. It would be like denying our hands their natural office. They would revolt. They would not remain in our pockets or behind our backs or toying with a button. We should have to chain them up, so instinctive and impetuous is their impulse to leap at a brother hand.

No doubt the custom has its disadvantages. We all know hands that we should prefer not to shake, warm, clammy hands, listless, flaccid hands, bony,

On Shaking Hands

energetic hands. The horror and loathing with which Uriah Heep filled our youthful mind was conveyed more through the touch of his hand than by any other circumstance. It was a cold, dank hand that left us haunted with the sense of obscene and creepy things. I know the touch of that hand as though it had lain in mine, and whenever I feel such a hand now the vision of a cringing, fawning figure damns the possessor of it in my mind beyond reprieve. It may be unjust, but the hand-clasp is no bad clue to moral as well as physical health. "There is death in that hand" was Coleridge's remark after parting from Keats, and there are times when we can say with no less confidence that there is pollution, or dishonesty, or candour, or courage "in that hand."

Some personalities seem to resolve themselves into a hand-shake. It is so eloquent that it leaves nothing more to be discovered about them. There is Peaker, the publisher, for example, who advances with outstretched hand and places it in yours as though it is something he wants to get rid of. It is a cold pudding of a hand, or a warm pudding of a hand, according to the weather, but, cold or warm, it is equally a pudding. What are you to do with it? It obviously doesn't belong to Peaker, or he would not be so anxious to get rid of it. You can't shake it, for it is as unresponsive as a jelly-fish, and no one can shake hands heartily with a jelly-fish. Hand-shaking must be mutual, or it is not at all. So you just hold it as long as civility demands, and then gently return it to Peaker, who goes and tries to get someone else to take it off his hands, so to speak.

On Shaking Hands

And at the other extreme is that hearty fellow
Stubbings, the sort of man who

> Hails you "Tom" or "Jack,"
> And proves by thumping on your back
> How he esteems your merit.

But he does not thump you on the back. He takes
your hand—if you are foolish enough to lend it to
him—and crushes it into a jumble of aching bones
and shakes your arm well-nigh out of its socket.
That's the sort of man I am, he seems to say. Nothing
half-hearted about me, sir. Yorkshire to the back-
bone. Jannock right through, sir. (Oh, torture!) And
I'm glad to see you, sir. (Another jerk.) He restores
your hand, a mangled pain, and you are careful not
to trust him with it again at parting. And there is
the limp and lingering hand that seems so overcharged with affection that it does not know when to
go, but lies in your palm until you feel tempted to
throw it out of the window. But though there are
hands that make you shudder and hands that make
you writhe, the ritual is worth the occasional penalty
we have to pay for it. It is the happy mean between
the Oriental's formal salaam and the Russian's
enormous hug, and if it has less dignity than the
Arab's touch with the finger-tips, which is like a
benediction, it has more warmth and more of the
spirit of human comradeship. We shall need a lot of
medical evidence before we cease to say with the
most friendly of all poets:

> Then here's a hand, my trusty frien',
> And gie's a hand o' thine.

ON A FINGER-POST

AT the end of the orchard, where the road that climbs up the hillside from the valley crosses the old British track that had ambled along the slopes of the hills for thousands of years, stands a finger-post. One of its hands has fallen with age, and the other two are hardly legible, though with difficulty you may see that one of them directs the wayfarer to Dunstable. I have never seen anyone consult it, and on a moonlight night it looks the most gaunt and solitary thing on earth, for ever pointing a minatory finger over the glimmering landscape, like a prophet vainly directing a naughty and unheeding world to the land of Beulah. Nobody takes any notice of it.

But it has its moments of consequence. On high-days and holidays in the summer, days such as these, happy picnickers from afar, mostly school-children out for their annual treat, come to a halt at the old finger-post on their way to the summit of the hill. The horses are unhitched from the waggonette and are left to graze while the children spread their lunch or their tea on the Icknield Way, which here resumes the character of a green-ride over which the centuries have passed without record of change. But no one ever seems to want to go to Dunstable. I do not want to go to Dunstable myself. In time I suppose the poor old finger-post will tire of telling

53

the world to go to Dunstable and will drop its second arm in weariness and despair.

I have no desire to go to Dunstable, because I like the name so much that I do not want to spoil the emotion of pleasure it gives me by any earthly contacts. I should as soon think of going to Dunstable as of going to Ashby-de-la-Zouch. I would not destroy the poetry that hangs about that name for anything the place could give me. Ashby-de-la-Zouch belongs to the realm of dreams, where high romance is always afoot and you may see any day some splendid knight in the tournament charging down upon his foe, while the beautiful heroine drops her handkerchief to show that she can bear no more. Why should I desecrate this agreeable fancy by discovering that Ashby-de-la-Zouch is (perhaps) a grubby little place with one frowsy tea-shop and a tin tabernacle? I do not say that that is what Ashby-de-la-Zouch is like. It may be a very nice place with a boulevard and a bandstand. I shall never know. But it could not possibly be like my Ashby-de-la-Zouch. Nothing could be like my Ashby-de-la-Zouch.

It is so with Bideford in Devon. It may be that if one went to Bideford in Devon one would find it very much like Southend-on-Sea, or Skegness or Blackpool or any other popular resort. It may have a pier and half-a-dozen cinemas and a "Ham and Eggs" Parade like New Brighton. It may be a wilderness of stuffy lodging-houses, with

"APARTMENTS"

in every window, and touts who salute you at every

On a Finger-Post

step. But to the imagination Bideford in Devon is something quite different from that. It is the gateway of adventure, the arch wherethrough gleams the untravelled world. On the shore you may meet Grenville or Drake in buff jerkin and silken hose, and Salvation Yeo telling tales to a crowd of open-mouthed youths and blowing clouds of tobacco before their astonished eyes. And in the harbour you may see the little *Revenge* herself, waiting for her crew of "men from Bideford in Devon" who are to share in the immortal exploit that hangs like an imperishable halo over this Devon shore.

I once knew a man who came from Bideford. I don't suppose he was really better than if he had come from Chowbent, or Wigan, or Coggeshall. I fancy he was quite an ordinary man; but to me he came trailing clouds of glory from afar. He seemed to waft breezes from the Spanish Main before him, and in his pockets I fancied I heard the chink of doubloons that had come from a treasure-ship in Nombre Dios Bay. I could not regard him as a man. I regarded him as a romance. What else could one do with a man who came from Bideford in Devon? I was very young then, but I doubt whether years have wrought any difference. I doubt whether I could do business with any success with a man who had come from Bideford. I should be as wax in his hands or as clay to the potter. But much as I love the sound of its name, no finger-post will ever tempt me to Bideford in Devon. I will preserve the vision. I will not break the spell.

Now, it is different with places like those Essex

villages, Messing and Mucking. Anyone might go to Messing or to Mucking and have quite a pleasant surprise. I have not been to them myself, but I should not be afraid to go to them. If Messing (or Mucking) should turn out to be no better than its name I should rejoice in its blunt honesty, and if on the contrary it should prove a country idyll, all ivy and parish pumps and village greens and thatched cottages, with perhaps the ancient pound in one field and the old village stocks in another, a ghost haunting the Tudor manor-house and an owl keeping its nightly vigil in the church tower—if, I say, Messing (or Mucking) should be like this one, one would have the sensation which Mr. Birrell had when he picked up a first edition of Gray's *Elegy* on a threepenny barrow. Yes, decidedly, if that finger-post pointed to Messing or Mucking I would go there. But not to Dunstable.

Places with beautiful or suggestive names are like the heroes of our fancy: they ought not to be seen. Who ever saw a man who had become a myth to him without disappointment? I remember when I was a boy and saw W. G. Grace for the first time what a sense of disillusion I suffered. He had become a fable to me. I used to see him in imagination descending from Olympus, with all nature celebrating his advent. The clouds would clap their hands at his approach and the earth would assuredly tremble with joy. And instead he just walked about and talked like any other man, and got out on the same plane of frail mortality. It was my first lesson in the brutal realism of things.

It was such a shock that Stevenson records in

On a Finger-Post

Across the Plains. Who is there who has not felt the beauty of that word "Wyoming"? It is a name that would almost make one forget the toothache. It is the very stuff of poetry, a balm for the troubled spirit, an anodyne for the jangled nerves. I could imagine a doctor prescribing that a patient should repeat "Wyoming" half a dozen times every hour as a cure for neurasthenia or something like that. That was how Stevenson felt about it until he had the misfortune to see it.

To cross such a plain (Nebraska) is to grow homesick for the mountains. I longed for the Black Hills of Wyoming, which I knew we were soon to enter, like an ice-bound whaler for the spring. Alas! and it was a worse country than the other. All Sunday and Monday we travelled through these sad mountains or over the main ridge of the Rockies, which is a fair match to them in misery of aspect. Hour after hour it was the same unhomely and unkindly world about our onward path. . . .

But get down the book and read the whole passage. It is as beautiful a piece of descriptive prose as you will find anywhere. But when you have read it you will be glad that you have not been to Wyoming and that you can still soothe the toothache with the sound of its magic name.

I shared the disenchantment which Stevenson felt in Wyoming when not long ago I travelled by the Ohio. I had been a captive since childhood to those bewitching vowels. However dull the world seemed, it could be brightened by the thought of the Ohio. I saw that shining river flowing through the landscape of fancy to the Southern seas, to the accompaniment of negro melodies and the song of the mocking-bird.

On a Finger-Post

Its waters were crystal like the river of Bunyan's vision, and as they went they sang of the old legends of the Kentucky Shore and Tennessee. Now the vision is shattered. I know that the Ohio (in winter at all events) is as yellow as pea-soup and as thick, flowing by rank, dishevelled shores, slopping over its banks and leaving great messy pools along its borders. I travelled by it and across it for the best part of a day, and I left it behind as gratefully as Stevenson left behind the Black Hills of Wyoming. It was a warning to me to leave the cloud palaces of the mind unvisited. If I ever see a finger-post pointing to Wyoming, I shall ignore it as I ignore the hand that, from the corner of the orchard, points me to Dunstable.

THE OPEN WINDOW

I ENTERED a railway-carriage at a country station the other morning and found myself in a compartment containing five people. I took a vacant seat between a man in the corridor corner and a lady dressed in handsome furs in the window corner. A girl whom I took for the lady's daughter sat opposite to her, and a gentleman whom I took to be the lady's husband sat next the girl, while another man occupied the remaining corner by the corridor. These people had all evidently been in the train some time, and on entering I was vaguely sensible of having broken in upon a drama which was unfinished. The atmosphere seemed charged with feelings whose expression had only been suspended, and I was not surprised when, the train being in motion, hostilities were resumed.

The window by which the lady sat was half-open, and as the train gathered speed the wind, which was blowing from the east, came in like a whip-lash. It missed the lady in her wraps, but hit me in the face and curled round the neck of the man in the corridor corner. He leaned forward and asked, with the air of having made the request before, that the window should be closed. "Certainly not!" said the lady. I glanced at her and, so far as her face was visible above the billowing furs that enveloped her, saw she

was a person who was not to be trifled with. Her
lips were tight pressed and her nostrils swelled
with battle.

The man in the corner addressed himself to the
husband, who had buried himself in his newspaper
in the obvious hope of being overlooked. The man
explained with what deadly aim the wind came into
his corner, and how if the window were shut and the
corridor door was opened they could have plenty
of air without discomfort. Dragged thus into the
fighting-line, the husband lowered his paper and
looked over his glasses timidly in the direction of his
wife. She had a copy of a picture paper in her hands,
and without looking at her husband she emitted a
little snort and turned the pages as if she were wring-
ing their necks. The husband, who had a kindly face
and looked as though he had long since laid down
his arms in an unequal battle, knew the symptoms.
He uttered no word to the terrific woman by the
window, but turning to the man and still looking
benignly over his glasses, offered to take the post of
peril in the corner. The man said No, he was quite
comfortable in his corner if the window were closed.
He put on his hat, turned up his coat collar, held
up his paper against the gale and fell silent.

The husband, with one more furtive glance at his
wife, resumed reading. As I watched him I thought
of the story of the old parson, who, driving with his
wife in a country lane, met a farmer in his cart. There
was no room to pass, and the law of the road made
the parson the offender. It was his business to "back"
to a wide place in the lane to allow the farmer's cart

The Open Window

to pass. But the parson's wife would not let him do so. The farmer must get out of the way. The poor parson was in tears between his duty and terror of his wife. "Don't worry, parson; don't worry," said the farmer. "I'll go back. I've just such a old varmint as her myself at home."

And that was how the battle over the window ended. The man in the corner made one brief rally. He flung the corridor door open in the hope of diverting the draught or, perhaps, making things unpleasant for his foe. But she was invulnerable to attack. She only stabbed the pages of her picture paper a little more viciously. The man then fled from the field. He went out and found seats for himself and his companion in another compartment, and returning removed his luggage. The lady's victory was complete. She was left unchallenged mistress of the compartment. She gave her paper a final comprehensive stab, commanded her husband to close the corridor door which her defeated antagonist had shamelessly left open, and sat up to enjoy her triumph.

As I looked from her to the nice, kindly, hen-pecked husband now again absorbed in his newspaper, I felt pity for so afflicted a fellow-creature. Poor fellow! What a life!

ON AN UNPOSTED LETTER

I took a bundle of old letters out of a jacket pocket this morning to look for a document which I wanted, and which I thought might be there. It was not there. I was not in the least surprised. I am never surprised when I do not find things in my pockets. Long experience has taught me not to expect to find what I want in my pockets and what ought to be there. But, on the other hand, I rarely fail to find things I do not want, things that simply refuse to be lost, negligible things, tiresome things, old bills, old envelopes of vanished letters, notes I have made about matters long since dead, sometimes startling things that make me leap up with ejaculations only wrung from me in moments of sudden dismay.

It was so this morning. For though I did not find the document I wanted, I found a couple of letters, written a fortnight ago, put in envelopes, addressed and stamped—but not posted. One of them was of little consequence: the other was of much consequence. It was to a person who, I knew, expected to hear from me on an important matter, and from whom I had expected to hear in reply. I had wondered why he had not replied, and why when he saw me at a club a few days ago he rather obviously avoided me. I felt puzzled, for there had been nothing in my

On an Unposted Letter

letter at which he could take offence—yet obviously he had taken offence. Now I knew why he had taken offence. He was annoyed at not receiving a letter from me which he had expected to receive, and I was annoyed at not receiving a reply to a letter I had not sent.

And in this little incident I saw an illustration of most of the personal differences which afflict us in our journey through this troublesome life. Take a common example. A is talking to B as they walk along the street on a subject of absorbing interest to him when C passes them. A knows C quite well, and in ordinary circumstances would give him a cordial greeting, but he is so full of his argument with B that he is only dimly conscious of C's propinquity and he passes with a vague air of having seen him in another world. A has no intention of being rude or even distant, and goes on without the least idea that he has given C offence. Indeed, he is not aware that he has seen C, so deep was he in thought about other things. But C is a proud fellow, ready to feel an affront, and resolute in paying it back. The next time they meet C is stiff and remote and A goes away wondering why the fellow cut him and determined to be something of an iceberg himself when the occasion arises. And so from this trivial incident A and C drift into an attitude of hostility and aloofness which a moment's candour on either side would show to have no shadow of foundation.

Most of the actions of other people which give us annoyance spring from causes that have nothing to do with the motives we assign to them. Othello

On an Unposted Letter

smothers Desdemona through a misunderstanding about a handkerchief that five minutes' quiet talk would have cleared up, with disastrous results to the villain, Iago. It is an excellent rule to distrust our reading of facts, still more our reading of other people's motives in relation to them. It is wrong in nine cases out of ten. I can hardly recall a case in which my first conclusion as to why So-and-So did this or that has not, on fuller knowledge, turned out to be absurdly wide of the mark. How can it be otherwise? How, for example, can that excellent person who avoided me at the club know that I have not been guilty of an act of wilful discourtesy towards him? He does not know that the nice letter I wrote to him has been lying in one of my pockets for a fortnight. I did not even know it myself. Yet the knowledge of that fact is essential to a true understanding of my conduct towards him. He has doubtless smothered me under the pillow, Othello-fashion, as a rude fellow. It is a mistake. I am only a careless fellow who ought not to be trusted with such treacherous things as pockets.

I think the moral of it all is summed up in the remark which an intrepid lady, whose name has of late become a household word, once made to me. "I never allow misunderstandings to go unexplained," she said. "If a friend 'cuts' me I ask her why she cut me, and I usually find it is for a reason that does not exist. If I don't understand the action of a friend I ask for an explanation, and I generally find it clears the air." It is a good rule. If we were not too proud to explain ourselves or to ask explanations of others

On an Unposted Letter

most of the misunderstandings of life would disappear, and many of our worries with them.

In the meantime, I have posted that letter, with a covering note of explanation. That will remove one misunderstanding from my own encumbered path.

A NOTE ON DRESS

I READ a sensational article in a newspaper the other evening. It was an article which set forth Fourteen Commandments to men on how to be dressy. I call it sensational because of its novelty. Every day in almost any paper you turn to, you will find a page or half-page about women's dress, usually adorned by amazing drawings of impossible women dressed in impossible clothes, and standing in impossible attitudes, who all seem alike in their vacuity and futility. But never before do I remember to have seen in a daily newspaper an article addressed to men, telling them what clothes they should wear and how to wear them. I daresay there have been such articles, but I have not seen them, and certainly they are so infrequent that they may be said to be unknown.

I shall be curious to see whether the innovation has come to stay, for it has been a subject of mild speculation with me why all the literature of dress should be confined to women. On the face of it we might suppose that it was only women who wore clothes at all, and certainly only women who cared what clothes they wore or made a science of wearing them. No doubt this is largely true. Every woman has a serious interest in dress. "There was never fair woman but she made mouths in a glass," says the poet, and there was never woman of any sort, fair or plain, that could refuse at

A Note on Dress

least the tribute of a glance at a well-dressed milliner's window. You will hear women discuss dress on the bus as earnestly and continuously as their boys discuss cricket, or their husbands discuss stocks and shares, or motor-cars, or golf, or the iniquities of politicians. I have never yet heard two men discuss dress in the abstract for two minutes. You might sit in any smoking-room in any men's club in London for a year without hearing a remark on the fashion in ties or trousers, or a single comment on the fact that this or that person was well- or ill-dressed. If dress is mentioned at all, it is mentioned in an ironical vein, as a matter fitting, perhaps, for a light jest among friends, but nothing more.

This must not be taken to mean, I think, that men are wholly indifferent to dress. It does not fill anything like the place in their mind that it fills in the mind of women, and I fancy there is an unwritten convention among them that it is bad form almost bordering on the improper to talk about clothes. It would smack of vanity in regard to one's personal appearance. Women can talk about clothes without this sense of personal vanity. They talk about it in a detached, abstract way, as they might talk about pictures, or music, or any other æsthetic subject. They are interested in it objectively as an art. They like to see pretty dresses, even though they cannot hope to wear them. They throng to a wedding, not so much from interest in the principals as from the desire to see the clothes the bride wears. They like to see them much as they might like to hear a beautiful performance on the violin, although they them-

A Note on Dress

selves can never hope to play the violin. Even women who dress dowdily themselves and affect to have souls above the follies of their sex, secretly love a display of fashions and like to read about the garments of women they do not know and do not want to know.

Men are certainly not like this. They are not interested in dress as an art. If their newspaper, describing a political meeting, informed them that the chairman was dressed in a frock-coat, with three buttons and a full skirt, that he wore trousers with a tendency to bell-bottoms, and patent leather shoes with pointed toes, and white gaiters—if they were told this they would wonder what the joke was about. Where a man is keenly interested in dress, he is interested in his own dress. His concern is his own personal appearance. He is particular about the crease in his trousers and the cut of his coat where his wife, perhaps, is only interested in the objective beauty of gowns and toques, and can enjoy the sight of them on other people as well as in her own mirror.

Are we to conclude that men are superior to women in having none of this disinterested enthusiasm for dress as an art? It is a nice question. I should not wish to see the subject fill so large a place in their thought as it does in the case of women; but they ought not to be above it, or pretend that they are above it. After all, to be well-dressed—not "dressy" —nor necessarily fashionable—is as proper a wish in man as in woman. Dress has its spiritual and moral reactions. It may seem absurd, but it is true that we are in a real sense the creatures of our clothes. We are

A Note on Dress

better men, more civilised men, in a well-fitting garment than in an ill-made garment. Baggy knees dispirit the mind. Slovenliness does not stop at the clothes, but infects the soul. That is why a clean-up in the evening and a change of clothes is a good moral tonic for anyone. The case was well put by an Australian squatter to a friend of mine who visited him on his estate far away in the wilds of the interior. My friend asked him why, in so remote a place, he made it a practice to "dress" for dinner. "I do it," said the squatter, "to avoid losing my self-respect. If I did not dress for dinner I should end by coming in to dinner in my shirt-sleeves. I should end by not troubling to wash. I should sink down to the level of the cattle. I dress for dinner, not to make myself pretty, but as a spiritual renovation."

FAREWELL TO HAMPSTEAD

In the house there are portents of impending change. A feeling of clearance is in the air. There is a going-away aspect about the furniture, pictures are down and in odd passages and corners there are bundles and boxes of books piled up for removal. Most conclusive of all, there is beside the gate a board bearing in large red letters the word "Sold." It is the announcement to the world that I am on the march to fresh woods and pastures new. They are beautiful woods and desirable pastures. I have no doubt I shall be as happy amidst them as a very variable temper permits me to be in this very variable world of ours.

And yet I confess that the sight of that word "Sold" over the gate gives me an orphaned feeling. It translates itself in my mind into "Finis"—the end of a chapter, the completion of another long stage in a journey that seems now unconscionably short, the cold epitaph of irrevocable things. Taking farewell of a house that has become as familiar to you as your own shadow is like taking leave of something of your spiritual self. It is no longer a thing of bricks and mortar. It is compact of dreams and babbles of a thousand forgotten things that were and will not be again. That is so of any house where you have lived long and seen happy days; but when that house is at Hampstead, a bow-shot from the Heath, the twinge of parting is peculiarly sharp.

Farewell to Hampstead

I daresay there are as pleasant places under the sun as Hampstead. I do not know them, but I am willing to believe that there are. Pleasanter places, I think, there cannot be. It was Happy Hampstead in the far-off days when the Abbot and monks of Westminster used to come hawking and hunting up its breezy heights and down into the Forest of Middlesex beyond; it was Happy Hampstead when the gallants and fine ladies of two hundred years ago came to Well Walk to drink the waters and dance and philander in the greenwood, and it is Happy Hampstead still, the hill of vision and the inexhaustible playground of the city that spreads, vast and mysterious, at its foot. Here on this sandy spit, with its ponds and its hollows, its birch woods and its hawthorn bushes, its wide vistas and secret places, its sense of the seashore and its feeling of the mountains, is the land where it is always afternoon. Romance clings to it like an odour and mirth is in its very atmosphere. It is the idyll of London.

And what a wealth of memories swarm around its hillsides, peopling its quaint courts and ways, and the very gorse bushes, with the shadows of the past. There is hardly a foot of its soil that is without its story—Dick Turpin riding on moonlit nights over the swarthy heath; Dick Steele taking refuge from his creditors in the lonely cottage on Haverstock Hill, where Sir Charles Sedley had lived before him; the famous Kit-Cat Club with Addison and all the wits of the day holding its summer sessions hard by the Whitestone Pond; Charles Lamb hunting among the gorse bushes for the snuff-box that he had thrown away the

Shakes. and Stratford.
Dodsworth - Lakes

Farewell to Hampstead

day before in a mood of renunciation after a visit with Home to the "Bull and Bush"; Shelley carrying a poor woman whom he had found lying in the snow to Leigh Hunt's house in the Vale of Health; Sir Harry Vane coming out of his house on Rosslyn Hill on his last journey to the Tower; Constable's pines by the Spaniards' Road, and the gibbet tree on which the highwaymen were hanged in chains, that still lies where it fell above the road at North End; Wordsworth walking up the hill to visit Joanna Baillie; and Pope hobnobbing with Arbuthnot; Johnson, in the days of his poverty, tramping up from Fleet Street to see his ailing wife at Frognal; the tales of the Spaniards' Inn, where Mrs. Bardell had her party, and where the rioters assembled for their attack on Mansfield at Ken Wood; the great Pitt, in his madness at Pitt House; Romney nursing his gloomy spirit at Holly Hill; Keats attending his dying brother in Well Walk and writing his immortal odes in Wentworth Place; Crabbe——

But no, the shadows crowd too thick and fast to be recorded. I walk amongst them with the feeling that I, too, seem about to become a shadow, and as I leave the Heath where the children are playing hide-and-seek among the hawthorn trees and the dogs are splashing in the Leg of Mutton Pond and turn into a road where the one brazen word "Sold" seems to fill the landscape, I have a vague sense of attending a funeral. Fortunately it is my own funeral —the funeral of twenty happy years on this sunny eminence—and not the funeral of Happy Hampstead. Men may come and men may go, but neither

Farewell to Hampstead

time nor change can touch the spirit of this enchanted hill.

Jane says that she will never have the heart to return to it. I feel a bit like that myself. I feel that I shall not want to disturb the dream into which those Hampstead days are fading. It will be enough to remember that I too once dwelt in Arcady.

ON PLAGIARISM

I HAVE had many literary enthusiasms, some of them transient, some of them lasting, but Pope was never one of them. He seems to me to dwell in a walled-in garden, very perfectly kept, amazingly neat and tidy with the box-hedges trimmed to a nicety and shaped here and there into cocks and other fantasies; but airless and stuffy. I like to take a stroll down his trim couplets now and then, but I am soon content to pass out to the landscapes where the Miltons and Shelleys and Wordsworths and Shakespeares fill the lungs with the great winds and feast the eye with the great spaces. I do not therefore feel any particular horror at Professor Karl Pearson's discovery that Pope is a plagiarist. I should not be disturbed if he proved he was a bad plagiarist. He has not done that, but he has found that Pope's aphorism, "The proper study of mankind is Man," is lifted from Pierre Charron—"La vraye science et le vray estude de l'homme c'est l'Homme." It seems to me a rather poor, pedestrian thing to steal—so commonplace indeed as to defy paternity. Anybody might have said it without feeling that he had said something that anybody else could not have said as well.

If this were the worst charge of plagiarism that could be brought against Pope—and I shall show

On Plagiarism

presently that it is not—few illustrious poets would have so clean a record. If we damned him for so trivial a theft as this, what sort of punishment would be left for the colossal borrowings of a Shakespeare or a Burns? Take, for example, that most exquisite of Burns's songs, "O, my luve is like a red, red rose." There is not a single stanza that is not lifted from old ballads and chapbooks. Compare, as an illustration, the third stanza:

> Till a' the seas gang dry, my dear,
> And the rocks melt wi' the sun!
> And I will luve thee still, my dear,
> While the sands o' life shall run.

with this from *The Young Man's Farewell to his Love* in the Motherwell collection of chapbooks:

> The seas they shall run dry,
> And rocks melt into sands;
> Then I'll love you still, my dear,
> When all those things are done.

Even the fine change from "melt into sands" to "melt wi' the sun" is traceable to another source. Wordsworth and Milton, proud and austere though they were, were not above enriching their verse with borrowed thoughts. Milton's borrowings from Dante are abundant, but they are done in the grand manner, as of a prince taking a loan from an equal, not because he needs it, but as a token of their high companionship and their starry discourse. To be plagiarised by Milton would be no grievance, but a crowning distinction. It would be a title-deed for immortality. The two most beautiful lines in the poem on the

On Plagiarism

daffodils by Ullswater are Dorothy Wordsworth's, and in sending *The Ettrick Shepherd* to the *Athenæum* for publication Wordsworth acknowledged that in the lines:

> Like clouds that rake the mountain-summits
> Or waves that own no curbing hand.

he was indebted to a now unknown poet, G. Bell, who in speaking of Skiddaw said, "Yon dark cloud *rakes* and shrouds its noble brow." One can imagine G. Bell being famous in the Elysian Fields as the man from whom Wordsworth once borrowed a thought.

The indebtedness of Keats to others is indebtedness for words rather than ideas, but it is an immense debt. You can almost trace his reading by the perfumed words that he has ravished from other gardens, and to which he has given a new and immortal setting. When he writes: "Oh Moon! far-spooming Ocean bows to thee," we know that he has been dipping into Beaumont and Fletcher, and so we may track him through Milton and Spenser, Shakespeare and Chapman, Sandys' *Ovid* and Thomson's *Seasons*, and a score of other luxuriant gardens of long ago. But this plucking of verbal flowers can hardly come within the scope of plagiarism. For that accusation to hold there must be some appropriation of ideas or at least of rhythm and form. Often the appropriation may be so transfigured as to rob it of any element of discredit. Thus, Tennyson's:

> Our little systems have their day.
> They have their day and cease to be;
> *They are but broken lights of Thee,*
> And Thou, O Lord, art more than they.

On Plagiarism

is clearly traceable to the magnificent image in Shelley's *Adonais*:

> The One remains; the many change and pass;
> Heaven's light for ever shines, earth's shadows fly;
> Life, *like a dome of many-coloured glass*,
> Stains the white radiance of eternity
> Until Death tramples it to fragments.

In both we have the idea of Heaven's light streaming down upon the "broken lights" of our earthly tabernacle, and being splintered into many-coloured fragments, but the later poet's employment of the idea, however inferior, is sufficiently original and fresh to warrant the spoliation. And, indeed, Shelley himself must have had a great phrase of St. Augustine's in mind when he wrote his immortal stanza.

Often the apparent plagiarism is unintended, even unconscious. Some minds are tenacious of good things and quite honestly forgetful of the source. I don't refer to cases like that of the late Canon Fleming, who preached and published a sermon of Dr. Talmage's as his own, and when exposed declared that he had been so impressed by it that he had written it out and then forgotten it was not his own. Nor do I refer to such thefts as that of Disraeli from Thiers. In that case Disraeli, like Fleming, explained that he had copied the passage into his commonplace book and mistaken it for his own. But as Thiers did not speak English, the explanation, as Herbert Paul remarks, was not felt to be explanatory. I refer to honourable men who would not stoop to these depths of brazen effrontery. In the instance I have quoted from Tennyson, it is of course obvious that the poet

On Plagiarism

knew the source. He probably knew *Adonais* by heart, and he would certainly not have been shocked to find that others had noted the similarity. He quite deliberately invited criticism and comparison. In another case in which he appropriated a picturesque image from Shakespeare, it is difficult to suppose that he was unconscious of what he was doing. "Heigho! an it be not four by the day, I'll be hanged," says the Carrier, calling up the sleepy ostler in *Henry IV.*, "Charles's Wain is over the new chimney and yet our horse not packed. What, ostler!" In the *May Queen* we read:

And we danced about the maypole and in the hazel copse
Till Charles's Wain came out above the tall white chimney tops.

But, to take a recent instance, I do not imagine that Rupert Brooke was conscious of any indebtedness to Thoreau when he wrote:

Spend in pure converse our eternal day;
  Think each in each, immediately wise;
Learn all we lacked before; hear, know and say
  What this tumultuous body now denies;
And feel, who have laid our groping hands away ;
  And see, no longer blinded by our eyes.

Yet I do not think it would be possible to deny to these lines an indisputable echo of Thoreau's:

I hearing get who had but ears,
  And sight, who had but eyes before ;
I moments live, who lived but years,
  And truth discern who had but learning's lore.

It is conceivable that Brooke had not read Thoreau, though not probable. What is probable is that he had read the lines and that their vivid comparison of

On Plagiarism

physical and spiritual apprehension had taken seed in his fertile mind and germinated in due season.

It would not be easy for a man who wrote much to escape reminiscences of this sort. Even if he read nothing he would still inevitably hit on many ideas, similes, images, that others had used before him. The charge of plagiarism is only valid where the borrowing is deliberate and employed without creating new thought and new effects. Perhaps the most familiar illustration is that of Macaulay's New Zealander in the essay on Ranke's *History of the Popes*. It has been traced to many sources. It is found in Mrs. Barbauld and in Volney's *Ruins of Empires*. But the most exact parallel is this from Shelley's introduction to *Peter Bell the Third*:

Hoping that the immortality you have given to the Fudges you will receive from them; and in the firm expectation that when London is an habitation of bitterns; when St. Paul's and Westminster Abbey shall stand, shapeless and nameless ruins in the midst of an unpeopled marsh; when the piers of Waterloo Bridge shall become the nuclei of islets of reeds and osiers and cast the jagged shadows of their broken arches on the solitary stream; some transatlantic commentator, etc.

There is the whole vision complete, done in the spirit of comedy a generation before Macaulay dressed it in the pomp of his martial prose. Of course, Macaulay was familiar with the passage, and I assume he would have said that the idea was so exploited that it was common property which anybody was entitled to use who had a need and a use for it. And that is the best excuse that can be urged for most plagiarisms which are not mere cases of brazen theft or sheer

On Plagiarism

desecration. It is the latter offence which is the more inexcusable. Honest stealing may be defended; but to steal and to degrade is past forgiveness. What adequate punishment could one devise for that queer ornament of the Church, Warburton, who in his *Enquiry into the Causes of Prodigies and Miracles* could, half a century after the publication of the *Areopagitica*, write thus:

Methinks I see her, like a mighty eagle, renewing her immortal youth and purging her opening sight at the unobstructed benign meridian Sun who some pretend to say had been dazzled and abused by an inglorious pestilential meteor; while the ill-affected birds of night would with their envious hootings prognosticate a length of darkness and decay.

If this banal nonsense is compared with Milton's original it will not be easy to deny it the distinction of being the most clumsy example of plagiarism on record. And Pope himself could not only plagiarise but belittle his plunder, as witness his appropriation of Jonson's fine lines:

> What beckoning ghost, besprent with April dew,
> Hails me so solemnly to yonder yew?

which he converts into:

> What beckoning ghost along the moonlight shade
> Invites my steps and points to yonder glade?

Mr. Kipling, who is not himself, I think, much given to borrowing from others, is the most unequivocal advocate of free trade in plagiarism:

> When 'Omer smote his bloomin' lyre,
> 'E 'eard men sing by land and sea,
> And what 'e thought 'e might require
> 'E went and took—the same as me.

On Plagiarism

Men knew he stole; 'e knew they knowed.
They never made no noise or fuss,
But winked at 'Omer down the road,
And 'e winked back—the same as us.

That may be the lawless law for the Olympians, but
it will not serve humbler folk. You must be a big man
to plagiarise with impunity. Shakespeare can take his
"borrowed plumes" from whatever humble bird he
likes, and, in spite of poor Greene's carping, his
splendour is undimmed, for we know that he can
do without them. Burns can pick up a lilt in any
chapbook and turn it to pure gold without a "by
your leave." These gods are beyond the range of our
pettifogging *meums* and *tuums*. Their pockets are so
rich that a few coins that do not belong to them are no
matter either way. But if you are a small man of
exiguous talents and endeavour to eke out your
poverty from the property of others you will discover
that plagiarism is a capital offence, and that the
punishment is for life. In literature—whatever the
case may be in life—there is one law for the rich and
another for the poor, and "that in the captain's but a
choleric word which in the soldier is flat blasphemy."

THE CASE OF DEAN INGE

WE now know, from his own lips, what is wrong with Dean Inge. Nature has denied him the sense of music. He can neither sing nor make a joyful noise. He knows but two tunes, *God Save the King* and *John Peel*, and even these he, apparently, only recognises from afar. All the rest of the universe of harmony is just a jumble of strange noises to him. The pealing of the organ and the thrilling song of the choristers convey nothing to his imprisoned soul as he sits in his stall at St. Paul's. The release of the spirit, that feeling of getting clear of the encumbering flesh and escaping to a realm where all the burden and the mystery of this unintelligible world seem like a rumour from afar, a tale of little meaning, never comes to him. Let us assume that the escape is an illusion. But what an illusion! What an experience to have missed! Can we wonder that the Dean is a sad man and utters mournful sounds?

Perhaps Shakespeare, with his passion for song, overshot the mark when he said that the man who has not music in his soul

Is fit for treasons, stratagems, and spoils.

But there is a measure of truth in the axiom. We like complete men—men with all their spiritual limbs as well as all their physical limbs. We like them to have humour as well as gravity, to be able to sing as well as sigh, to love work and to love play, and not to be

The Case of Dean Inge

shut off from any part of the kingdom of the mind. No doubt the Dean will point out that many very eminent men have shared his affliction, and we shall be bound to agree that it is dangerous to generalise in this matter, as in most things. I could conceive him making out a very good case for the non-musical brotherhood. There is, of course, the leading instance of that most human and beautiful of spirits, Charles Lamb, who was even more deficient than the Dean, for he did not know *God Save the King*. But then, unlike the Dean, he had the desire to sing. The spirit was there, but it could find no utterance. He had tried for years, he tells us, to learn *God Save the King*, humming it to himself in quiet corners and solitary places, without, according to his friends, coming "within several quavers of it." No, I do not think, on second thoughts, that we can allow the Dean to claim St. Charles. He was a trier, like Mr. Chesterton. No one would suggest that Mr. Chesterton was musical, but he has the spirit of song in him and in a chorus he is splendid. He emits an enormous and affable rumble that suggests an elephant doing a cake-walk, or large lumps of thunder bumping about irrelevantly in the basement of the harmony.

But the Dean may have Southey. He is surrendered freely and ungrudgingly. He certainly had no feeling for music and no desire to feel it. "You are alive to know what follows," he says, describing a play, "and lo!—down comes the curtain and the fiddles begin their abominations." The fiddles begin their abominations! Take Bob Southey out, good Dean, and relieve us of his unctuous presence. And I am afraid we must

83

The Case of Dean Inge

let the Dean have Scott, too, though I part with him
with sorrow. "I do not know and cannot utter a
note of music," wrote Sir Walter; "and complicated
harmonies seem to me a babble of confused though
pleasing sounds." Pleasing, you observe. I am not
sure that we cannot snatch Sir Walter from the Dean's
clutches after all. We must part with Tennyson and
Ruskin, neither of whom had the sense of music, and
with Macaulay, who could only recognise one tune—
The Campbells are Coming. But we cannot let the Dean
have Coleridge, for though he disclaimed any understanding of complicated harmonies, he admits that
he loved to hear Beethoven, and the man who could
appreciate Beethoven a hundred years ago must not
go in the Dean's gloomy galley.

Nor shall old Sam Johnson go there, though he
confessed that he was insensible to the power of music.
"I told him," says Boswell, "that it affected me to
such a degree as to agitate my nerves painfully,
producing in my mind alternate sensations of pathetic
dejection, so that I was ready to shed tears, and of
daring resolution, so that I was inclined to rush into
the thickest part of the battle. 'Sir,' said he, 'I should
never hear it if it made me such a fool.'" But I
claim Samuel on the ground that during the tour
in the Hebrides he heard with rapt attention the
performance of the *Lament of the Scalded Cat*, and
still more because at Ashbourne he listened patiently
to a great number of tunes on the fiddle, and desired
to have *Let ambition fire thy mind* played over again.
It is a small thing, I own—a trivial ground on which
to claim him. I have never heard *Let ambition fire thy*

The Case of Dean Inge

mind, but the incident shows that Johnson had the root of the matter in him. Would the Dean, or Bob Southey, have asked to have *Let ambition fire thy mind* played over again? Would they have listened with rapt attention to *The Lament of the Scalded Cat*? Not they.

But even in the case of the Dean there is one pale, watery gleam of light in the general gloom. He knows *John Peel*. In his sombre heart that jolly song perhaps wakens some latent emotion of joy. It may be that with that key to the prison he might yet be rescued from his dungeon and turned into a happier man. Why should not the choir of St. Paul's try to convert him? Let them step across the Churchyard at night to the Dean's recess and ask in resonant chorus—

> D'ye ken John Peel wi' his coat so grey?
> D'ye ken John Peel at the break of day?
> D'ye ken John Peel when he's far, far away
> With his hounds and his horn in the morning?

and go on asking until the Dean comes to the window with the response—

> Yes, I ken John Peel, and Ruby too,
> Ranter and Ringwood, Bellman and True,
> From a find to a check, from a check to a view,
> From a view to a death in the morning.

And now, gentlemen, the chorus, if you please—all together:

> For the sound of his horn called me from my bed, etc.

It would be a great night in St. Paul's Churchyard, and it might do the Dean good. And we should all rejoice to hear him make a joyful noise for a change, even though it could not be called music.

A TALE OF FLEET STREET

No doubt there were greater things in Sir James Barrie's speech to the undergraduates at St. Andrews than the story of his conquest of Fleet Street; but for me, as for many others, there was nothing so interesting. It touched old chords of memory. There are many who have shared Sir James's youthful struggles without sharing his dazzling triumphs. My own thoughts went back more than forty years ago, about the time when Barrie came to London to try his luck in the enchanted street. I recalled two brothers—I knew them well—living in a country town, whose eyes were fixed on the starry realm of Fleet Street from afar. What a remote, impossible, golden world it seemed! Once they had known a fellow that had gone into it. He had been as one of themselves, familiar, companionable, ordinary; but one incredible day he had flown away to Fleet Street as naturally as a bird flies home to its nest, and they remained behind to imagine the sea of glory into which he had passed.

Then one day something happened. The younger of the two boys, Jonathan, noticed that the family copy of the *Standard* (that fine old paper that perished so lamentably of Tariff Reform) had been cut. An article, a column in length, had disappeared from the leader page. His curiosity was awakened. There was only one person in the household who was likely to have done this thing, and that was his brother,

A Tale of Fleet Street

Geoffrey. But to ask Geoffrey about it was impossible. He was a reticent person, who did not throw his confidences about, least of all among younger brothers. But Jonathan knew that he had been writing in the privacy of his bedroom late at night, and suspected that something had come of it. So he went out and purchased another copy of the *Standard*, turned to the column that had been missing, and there saw an article:

On a Country Corn Exchange
From a Correspondent

Ah! so he had done it, thought Jonathan. He had got his foot in the famous street with the golden pavements. That night he observed Geoffrey with a new feeling of importance, and saw him retire early to his bedroom with the delightful sense of sharing his great secret without his knowledge.

After that he waited for the *Standard* as eagerly as Geoffrey. He came to know the symptoms of an approaching event, and when he saw his brother cling to the *Standard* at breakfast and disappear with it into the garden, he knew that it was not the cricket news only—important as that was to both of them in those days—that made the paper so absorbing, and that when it fell to him there would be a gap in its contents. Then he noticed that other papers began to have occasional gaps, and life became a thrilling pursuit of Geoffrey's adventures in Fleet Street.

But the pursuit was not enough. It whetted his appetite for adventures of his own, and he too began

A Tale of Fleet Street

to retire to his bedroom early and write long and late, until the door opened and a gentle voice would say, "Child, you ought to be in bed." I fancy it was poor stuff that Jonathan wrote, and Fleet Street showed a cold indifference to it. There was one article on *A Harvest Home* that grew worn and crumpled by many transits through the post. But the struggle was not in vain. One unforgettable day he opened an evening paper, and there—Lo! Behold! . . . And next morning the postman brought a letter from the editor of the paper, stating—could he believe his eyes?—that he would be glad to receive further articles of the same character from his contributor. The sun shone with extraordinary splendour that day, and the birds sang more joyously than they had ever sung before. Jonathan walked on air—with the astonishing letter in his pocket—and he felt that Nature was rejoicing with him.

It is an old tale of far-off, forgotten things, called to mind by the recollections of Sir James Barrie. Perhaps it is worth telling, for the encouragement of other youths whose eager eyes are turned, wisely or unwisely, towards Fleet Street. I have lost sight of one of the brothers for many years; but he came to some prominence, edited a famous paper, and told me that when he went into the office he found, seated at a humble desk, the youth whose wonderful translation to Fleet Street had once filled him with envy and longing. The other brother still writes. I fancy I recognise his hand sometimes in articles that still have the note of that much-travelled manuscript of the *Harvest Home*.

ON THE TOP NOTE

A PLEASANT-LOOKING young lady (whose name I
think was Pamela) sitting opposite me in the bus was
complaining to her companion that Reginald was so
dead-alive. You couldn't get him excited about
anything. He was most *frightfully* clever, of course
—a B.Sc. and all that sort of thing, don't you know;
but, oh, so *awfully* icy. You went to a theatre with
him, and you got most *tremendously* thrilled, and he
would say, "Yes, quite nice." Or you got him to read
a book that was simply ripping and that you had
wallowed in most terrifically, and he would say,
"Quite nice." She liked people to be enthusiastic.
It was most horribly disappointing when you were
simply boiling with excitement to hear someone say,
"Yes, quite nice." It made you feel *most awfully*
done in, don't you know. If people enjoyed themselves, why shouldn't they say they enjoyed themselves and let themselves "go" a bit? She always
let herself go.

I felt that I agreed with her on the main issue.
Reginald *was* aggravating. I felt that I knew Reginald.
I saw him going through life more than a little bored
with everything. There's nothing new and nothing
true, and no matter, he seems to say. Man delights
him not, nor woman neither. He is astonished at
nothing, amused by nothing, cheered by nothing.

On the Top Note

His mind has disciplined his emotions so effectually that they have ceased to have anything to do. He is superior to tears or laughter, and would refuse to be surprised even if he saw the lions by the Nelson Column suddenly stand up and roar for their dinner. As a moderately enthusiastic person, I sympathised with the young lady opposite about Reginald. I wished Reginald would let himself go a bit.

But then it seemed to me that a mist passed before my vision and that Reginald himself was sitting in the seat opposite talking to a friend about Pamela. He liked Pamela very much, he said, but really her gush got on his nerves. She was always on her top note. Everything was most frightfully good or most awfully jolly or most hideously bad. Why couldn't people express themselves reasonably and use words with some respect for their meaning? He wished someone would tell Pam not to shriek every time she opened her mouth. It was such a pity, because she really had a pretty mouth and was a nice girl.

And hearing (imaginatively) Reginald's view of the matter, I was bound to admit that he had a case too. For I share his dislike of these extravagances of speech with which our Pamelas express the warmth of their feelings and the poverty of their minds. I should like to remind Pamela of the caution which Johnson gave to Boswell. He had accompanied Bozzy to Harwich to see him embark for Utrecht. I happened to say, says Boswell, it would be terrible if he should not find a speedy opportunity of returning to London, and be confined in so dull a place.

" Johnson: Don't, sir, accustom yourself to use

big words for little matters. It would *not* be *terrible*, though I *were* to be detained some time here."

It may have occurred to Boswell that Johnson was hardly the person to rebuke the use of big words; but though Johnson loved long words he did not use wrong words. His sin was not the hysteria of speech, but the pedantry of speech. He liked the fine clothes of language and dressed his thoughts up in full-bottomed wig and ruffles. It was a curious weakness for so great a man whose natural expression was always simple and vigorous. His big words were an after-thought of the pedant imposed on the brief, energetic utterance that was natural to him, as when commenting on some work he said that it "had not wit enough to keep it sweet" and then, pulling himself together, blunted the edge of that swift, keen criticism by saying that "it had not vitality enough to preserve it from putrefaction." But though Johnson's big words blurred his thought, they did not misrepresent it. They deprived it of force, but not of precision. His rebuke to Boswell was in regard to the extravagance of the word for the occasion. It would have been annoying or inconvenient to be kept at Harwich, but it would not have been terrible.

But the modern habit is not a mere matter of excess, as in the case of Boswell. In the attempt to be emphatic, Pamela murders speech. If you pass her the mustard, she says "Thanks, awfully." If she has enjoyed her game of tennis, she says it has been "awfully jolly," and if she approves of a book, she declares it to be "frightfully good." I am old enough to remember when this verbal atrocity began to be used, and I have lived to see it become the accepted coinage of a certain kind of conversation. It began as a piece of affectation, and has ended as a desolating vulgarity.

I do not think that Reginald wants Pamela to be less enthusiastic. He only wants her to preserve some proportion in regard to things. He feels as Jamie Soutar, of Drumtochty, in Ian Maclaren's story, felt. Jamie had "a gift o' discreemination," and was distressed by the purple adjectives of Mr. Hopps, the little Cockney. When Mr. Hopps raved about the sunset, Jamie observed that it was "no bad."

"No bad!" said Mr. Hopps. "I call it glorious, and if it hisn't, then I'd like to know what his."

"Man," replied Soutar austerely, "ye'll surely keep ae word for the 21st o' Reevelation."

Had any native used such words as "magnificent" in Drumtochty there would have been an uneasy feeling in the glen; the man must be suffering from wind in the head, and might upset the rotation of crops, sowing his young grass after potatoes, or replacing turnip with beet.

Reginald would not expect Pamela to put so harsh a bridle as this upon her tongue. He would only suggest that she should be sparing of her superlatives and her enthusiasm, so that when she used them they conveyed some sort of meaning and some sense of value. And probably Pamela would find that in curing herself she had cured Reginald. He would let himself "go" a little more if she let herself "go" a little less. For his iciness is probably an attempt to moderate her tropical fervour.

TEA AND MR. BENNETT

I KNEW that my friend Mr. Arnold Bennett was
a handy man. It is his foible to do many things,
and he does most of them surprisingly well. The
villagers in the poem were left wondering how the
schoolmaster's small head "could carry all he knew";
and I have myself often idly wondered how Mr.
Bennett has managed to become an expert in so many
arts and crafts in the intervals of pouring out a stream
of books and plays that would alone seem the abundant occupation of all his waking hours. I suppose
the explanation is, first, that he has in an unusual
degree an industrious habit under iron discipline and
an orderly mind that parcels out its minutes as a miser
parcels out his gold; and, second, that he has a
devouring curiosity about life.

He is a taster of life. He goes about like a country
boy at a fair, taking a shy at every Aunt Sally, a ride
on every roundabout, a shot at every shooting-range.
The bearded woman delights him, and Punch and
Judy hold him as the glittering eye of the ancient
mariner held the wedding guest. He never grows tired
of the show. He keeps into middle age the juvenile
wonder which most of us lose when we lose our youth
—hence the unfailing freshness of his mind. He is
always interesting, because he is always interested.
I would trust him to get along on a desert island as

Tea and Mr. Bennett

comfortably as any living man. He would write his own books, pen his own criticisms, paint his own pictures, make his own music, sail his own boat, take his own physic, run his own farm, engross his own conveyance, drive his own car, cook his own dinner—probably cut his own hair. For he can explain to you why the barbers of Italy are superior to the barbers of France and wherein the Dutch barber fails to touch the highest pinnacle of his calling. And all these things he would do, not clumsily or grudgingly as one driven into a corner by cruel circumstance, but joyfully, as a boy on a picnic. He would rejoice that at last he could do things as they should be done, instead of having them done for him by others in ways in which they should not be done.

For example, he would be able to have a cup of tea worth drinking. I did not know, but I am not surprised to learn, that he is an artist with the tea-pot. "I would undertake," he has just told the world, "to make better tea than nineteen-twentieths of the housewives of this country." If it were anybody else, we should say this was conceit; but Mr. Bennett without this note of childlike self-assurance would not be the Mr. Bennett we love. We should not know him. We should think he was just an ordinary man like the rest of us, and pass him by in the crowd. Moreover, when he tells us that he is a master craftsman with the tea-pot, I have no doubt he is speaking the truth. He will, I am sure, have studied this great subject as profoundly as he has studied the technique of play-writing.

And I daresay he would agree that it is at least as

Tea and Mr. Bennett

well worth studying as play-writing. Plays are only a very occasional affair in our life, but tea flows on for ever. At this moment I hear the pleasant clatter of the tea-things in the next room, and I suppose there is hardly a house in the land where the kettle is not boiling and the cups are not tinkling. When I went to see my lawyer yesterday afternoon he rang for "another cup," and if I go to see my publisher to-morrow afternoon he will ring for "another cup," too. Next to the Russians, we are, I suppose, the greatest tea-topers in the world. Tea-drinking has ceased to be merely a custom and has become a ritual as well. It is what the pipe of reconciliation is to the Indian or the eating of salt is to the Mussulman.

Yet though every day we drink enough tea to float the British Navy, it is probably true, as Mr. Bennett suggests, that few of us know how to make it. I do not pretend to be one of the few. But I delight in the rare occasions on which I get the real article, and in a casual way, quite different I am sure from Mr. Bennett's orderly experiments, I have picked up the rudiments of a system from those whose brews have pleased me. Thus from one great artist of the tea-pot, a fine old gentleman with a long white beard, who used to sit and watch the kettle boiling as anxiously as the doctor feels the pulse of his patient, I learned that the water should be poured on the tea the moment it comes to the boil. From another, a learned scientist, I gathered that boiling water (from another kettle, I fancy) should be poured in the pot before the tea is put in. A bachelor acquaintance of mine, on whom I called one afternoon, indoctrinated

Tea and Mr. Bennett

me with the idea of washing the tea with a rapid
drench of boiling water drawn off instantly before
pouring in the water intended for the brew. From
another friend (this time a lady) I picked up the fact
that the way to weaken your tea is not to pour more
water into the tea-pot, but to dilute the beverage
in the cup.

A small matter you say; but the art of making tea
is composed of these small delicacies. What, for
example, could seem a matter of more indifference
than that of the order in which you pour the milk
and the tea in the cup? Yet it is a capital point. Put
the tea in first, and the virtue seems to have gone
out of the cup; put the milk in first, and the subtle
law of the art is observed. And the proportion of milk
must be exact; you cannot add to it afterwards and
get the same effect.

I pass by such fundamental points as the selection
of the right tea for the water and the duty of pouring
off the tea quickly so as to catch the first fine rapture
of the leaf. But I hope I have said enough to set
tongues wagging on this fruitful subject, and enough
to win the respect (perhaps even the envy) of Mr.
Arnold Bennett. I don't mind confessing that that
is the reason I am writing this article. I am weary of
the omniscience of Mr. Bennett. I am humiliated by
the sense of the number of things I don't know or
can't do when I am in his presence or read his books.
If I did not love him I should hate him. I should
write to the papers to denounce him as a charlatan.
I should guy his pictures and scoff at his books and
make fun of his criticisms about this, that and the

Tea and Mr. Bennett

other and quote slighting things about Jacks-of-all-trades and generally make myself unpleasant. But since I love him I content myself with saying firmly and even defiantly, that I have ideas on the art and science of tea-making, too. True, I have never made it, but I could make it at a pinch.

ON BUYING AND SELLING

JANET said that she had seen John Staunton in the village in his new car. He was very pleased with it, and apparently still more pleased that he had sold his old car just before the big reduction in the makers' prices was announced, with the result that he had got a new car for an old of the same make, and was some pounds in pocket into the bargain. "I should be ashamed to gloat over such a transaction," she said. Indeed, she was doubtful whether it was morally right to benefit in such a way.

I agreed that it was perhaps indecent to "gloat" over such a stroke of luck, but I could not agree that any reasonable moral consideration had been outraged by the affair. The question raised the problem of what is fair in the way of deals of this sort. What, for example, ought one to say of the case of the eminent statesman of these days, who, looking over the stock of a second-hand book-dealer, saw a copy of the first edition of Gray's *Elegy* marked at a few shillings, and bought it, took it away, and has probably got it to-day? He had got a prize worth, I think, in the neighbourhood of two hundred pounds. He knew its value, and apparently the bookseller did not. What was the "morality" in that case? Ought he to have summoned the bookseller and said, "My dear sir, are you aware that this little book which you offer

On Buying and Selling

me at the ridiculous price of a few shillings is worth
a couple of hundred pounds?" I think that would
be demanding too much of human nature. Book-
buying and bookselling is a business transaction like
any other, and it is the bookseller's business to
know what his stock is worth. All the same, I hope
the eminent statesman sent the bookseller a substantial Christmas box *without* telling him what a
fool he had been.

After all, the traffic in curiosities is a sort of sport
in which sometimes the seller and sometimes the
buyer wins the trick. I heard the other day an amusing
incident of a man who was fond of collecting old
furniture. He was walking in a remote country district
when the rain came on, and he took shelter in a barn,
at the door of which the farmer was standing. The
collector noticed in a corner of the barn an old
chest containing fodder of some sort. He looked at it,
saw that it was obviously very old, spoke to the
farmer about it, found he knew nothing of its value,
and bought it for a comparatively small sum. Not
long after a friend of his who knew of the bargain
wandered to the same farm in the hope of picking up
something for himself. He went into the barn and
there, behold! was another old chest, containing some
more old fodder. Only it wasn't an old chest. Like
the other, it was simply a modern-antique—a bait
for hungry trout to snap at. The farmer was just an
agent. He did not invite people to buy, and he did
not pretend that the pieces were old. He just sold
them at a price if they were asked for. Was he morally
culpable? Was he more culpable than the buyer

On Buying and Selling

would have been if he had taken advantage of the farmer's real instead of supposed ignorance?

If we applied the code of strict morality in these matters and asserted that no one must benefit by another's lack of knowledge, what would become of the Stock Exchange? It would have to close its doors forthwith. Nearly every transaction between a buyer and a seller is in the nature of a duel in which one backs his supposed knowledge against the other's supposed ignorance. If I have reason to know, let me say, that salt-water has got into the Mexican oil wells, is it wicked of me to sell out my shares in the company to some innocent person who does not possess that piece of information? After all, I may be wrong, and he may know more than I do. He may know that the menace was true, but he may have the later information that it has been overcome. Every transaction of this sort is admittedly a competition in knowledge or calculation, and each side takes the risk in the hope of taking the profit.

There are, of course, cases in which it would be dishonourable to profit by private knowledge. If I knew that a certain firm was going bankrupt and sold my shares in it to a man who could not possibly know and from whom I deliberately concealed my own absolute knowledge on the point, I should be guilty of an act which would not be morally distinguishable from theft. Or if I went into a remote house of a poor peasant, found a First Folio Shakespeare—think of it!—the market price of which is now over five thousand pounds, discovered that the peasant was ignorant of its value, and took it away

On Buying and Selling

for a pound or two, I should be morally, though not legally, a thief. Fortunately I shall never have such a temptation thrust on me. I wonder what I should do if I had.

The difference between such a case and that of the Gray's *Elegy* is that the seller in the latter case was a business man setting his knowledge against the buyer's, and in the other he would be an innocent who was being rooked. In the matter of John Staunton I see no question of impropriety. One chanced to sell luckily and the other to buy unluckily. That is all. But I agree with Janet that John oughtn't to have "gloated" openly over the transaction. He should have purred to himself privately.

ON BIG WORDS

I WAS cutting down the nettles by the hedge with a bill-hook when a small man with spectacles, a straw hat, a white alpaca jacket, and a book under his arm came up, stopped, and looked on. I said "Good evening," and he said "Good evening." Then, pointing to my handiwork, he remarked:

"You find the nettles very difficult to eradicate?"

I said I found them hard to keep down.

"They disseminate themselves most luxuriantly," he said.

I replied that they spread like the dickens.

"But they have their utility in the economy of Nature," he said.

I replied that Nature was welcome to them as far as I was concerned.

He then remarked that it was most salubrious weather, and I agreed that it had been a fine day. But he was afraid, he said, that the aridity of the season was deleterious to the crops, and I replied that my potatoes were doing badly. After that, I think it occurred to him that we did not speak the same language, and with another "Good evening" he passed on and I returned to the attack on the nettles.

It is an excellent thing to have a good vocabulary, but one ought not to lard one's common speech or everyday letters with long words. It is like going out

On Big Words

for a walk in the fields with a silk hat, a frock-coat, and patent leather boots. No reasonable person could enjoy the country in such a garb. He would feel like a blot on the landscape. He would be as much out of place as a guest in a smock-frock at a Buckingham Palace garden-party. And familiar conversation that dresses itself up in silk-hatted words is no less an offence against the good taste of things. We do not make a thing more impressive by clothing it in grand words any more than we crack a nut more neatly by using a sledge-hammer. We only distract attention from the thought to the clothes it wears. If we are wise our wisdom will gain from the simplicity of our speech, and if we are foolish our folly will only shout the louder through big words.

Take for example that remark of Dr. Johnson's about the swallows. "Swallows certainly sleep all the winter," he said. "A number of them conglobulate together, by flying round and round, and then all in a heap throw themselves under water and lie in the bed of a river." It was a foolish belief, but it would be unfair to scoff at Johnson for not being better informed than his contemporaries. It is that bumptious word "conglobulate" that does for him. It looks so learned and knowing that it calls attention to the absurdity like a college cap on a donkey's ears.

A fine use of words does not necessarily mean the use of fine words. That was the mistake which Humpty-Dumpty made in *Alice in Wonderland*. He thought that "impenetrability" was such a magnificent word that it would leave Alice speechless and amazed. Many writers are like that. When the reporter says that So-and-So "manipulated the ivories" (meaning that he had played the billiard-balls into position), or that So-and-So "propelled the sphere" (meaning that he had kicked the football), he feels that he has got out of the rut of common speech when in fact he has exchanged good words for counterfeit coin. That is not the way of the masters of language. They do not vulgarise fine words. They glorify in simple words, as in Milton's description of the winged host:

> Far off their coming shone . . .

Quite ordinary words employed with a certain novelty and freshness can wear a distinction that gives them not only significance but a strange and haunting beauty. I once illustrated the point by showing the effects which the poets, and particularly Wordsworth and Keats, extract from the word "quiet." Shakespeare could perform equal miracles with the trivial word "sweet," which he uses with a subtle beauty that makes it sing like a violin in the hands of a master. Who can be abroad in the sunshine and singing of these spring days without that phrase, "the sweet o' the year," carolling like a bird in the mind? It is not a "jewel five words long." It is a dewdrop from the very mint of Nature. But Shakespeare could perform this magic with any old word. Take "flatter." A plain, home-spun word, you would say, useful for the drudgery of speech but nothing more. Then Shakespeare takes it in hand, and it shines bright as Sirius in the midnight sky:

> Full many a glorious morning have I seen
> Flatter the mountain tops with sovran eye.

On Big Words

I once wanted to use for purposes of quotation a familiar stanza of Burns, but one word, the vital word, escaped me. I give the stanza, with the word I lacked missing:

> To make a happy fireside clime
> For weans and wife—
> That's the true   and sublime
> Of human life.

You, perhaps, know the missing word; but I could not recall it. I tried all the words that were serviceable, and each seemed banal and commonplace. I dare not, for shame, mention the words I tried to use as patches for Burns. When I turned up the poem and found that poignant word "pathos," I knew the measure of my failure to draw the poet's bow.

We carry big words in our head for the expression of our ideas, and short words in our heart for the expression of our emotions. Whenever we speak the language of true feeling, it is our mother tongue that comes to our lips. It is equal to any burden. Take the familiar last stanza of Wordsworth's: "Three years she grew in sun and shower":

> Thus Nature spake—the work was done—
> How soon my Lucy's race was run!
> She died, and left to me
> This heath, this calm and quiet scene;
> The memory of what has been,
> And never more will be.

It is so simple that a child might have said it, and so charged with emotion that a man might be forgiven if he could not say it. *A Shropshire Lad* is full of

this surge of feeling dressed in home-spun, as when
he says:

> Into my heart an air that kills
> From yon far country blows:
> What are those blue remembered hills,
> What spires, what farms are those?
>
> That is the land of lost content,
> I see it shining plain,
> The happy highways where I went
> And cannot come again.

Even in pictorial description the most thrilling
effects, as in the case I have quoted from Milton,
are produced not by the pomp of words but by the
passion of words. In two rapid, breathless lines:

> The sun's rim dips, the stars rush out,
> With one stride comes the dark,

Coleridge flashes on the mind all the beauty and
wonder of the tropic night. And though Shakespeare,
like Milton and Wordsworth, could use the grand
words when the purpose was rhetorical or decorative,
he did not go to them for the expression of the great
things of life. Then he speaks with what Raleigh
calls the bare intolerable force of King Lear's:

> Do not laugh at me,
> For as I am a man, I think this lady
> To be my child Cordelia.

The higher the theme rises the more simple and
austere becomes the speech, until the words seem
like nerves bared and quivering to the agony of
circumstance:

> *Lear.* And my poor fool is hanged! No, no, no life!
> Why should a dog, a horse, a rat, have life,
> And thou no breath at all? Thou'lt come no more,

On Big Words

Never, never, never, never, never!
Pray you, undo this button. Thank you, sir.—
Do you see this? Look on her, look, her lips,—
Look there, look there!   [*He dies.*

Edgar. He faints! My lord, my lord!—
Kent. Break, heart; I prithee, break!
Edgar. Look up, my lord.
Kent. Vex not his ghost: O let him pass! he hates him
    That would upon the rack of this tough world
    Stretch him out longer.

The force of words can no farther go. And my friend
in the white alpaca jacket will notice that they are
all very little ones.

DO WE BUY BOOKS?

I HAVE recently been in the throes of a double removal, and in the course of the operation comments were made by one person or another concerned in it on the prominence of books in my belongings. The van-man, with a large experience of removals, paid the tribute of astonishment at the spectacle, and the people who came to look at the house gaped at the books as though they were the last thing they expected to see in a decent suburban residence. Hitherto I had been rather ashamed of my library. In the course of a longish life I have accumulated some 2000 books. There is not much rubbish among them, for I have thinned them out periodically, but there are shameful blanks that are unfilled, and it had never occurred to me to think that they formed an unusual collection for a middle-class household.

But the inquiries I have made since lead me to the conclusion that they do, and that in the average suburban home the last thing that is thought about is the furnishing of a library. People who will spend many hundreds and even thousands of pounds in the course of years in making their house beautiful never give a serious thought to books. They will ransack London for suitable fittings, for rugs and hangings, china and cut-glass, mirrors and what-nots, but the idea of providing themselves with a moderate

Do We Buy Books?

and well-selected library does not occur to them. If they gather books at all they gather them haphazard and without thought. A well-known publisher told me the other day that he was recently asked to equip a library in a new house in North London, and the instruction he received was to provide books that would fit the shelves which had been fixed. It was not the contents of the books that mattered, but the size.

This was no doubt an exceptional case, but it does represent something of the attitude of the average man to books. People who will spend one hundred and fifty pounds on a piano as a matter of course will not spend ten pounds a year or even five pounds a year in enriching their homes with all the best thought of all time. Go into any average provincial town and the last thing you will find is a decent book-shop. I recall more than one great industrial town of a population of over a hundred thousand which has only one such shop, and that is generally kept going by the sale of school-books. It is not because we cannot afford to buy books. We spend two hundred millions sterling a year on beer, and I doubt whether we spend two hundred million pence on literature. Many people can afford to buy motor-cars at anything from two hundred pounds who would be aghast at the idea of spending half a guinea occasionally on a book. They think so meanly of their minds as that.

Yet, merely as furniture, books are a cheaper and better decoration than blue china or Chippendale chairs. They are better because they put the signature of individuality upon a house. The taste for Chippendale chairs and blue china may be a mere vanity,

Do We Buy Books?

a piece of coxcombry and ostentation, a fancy that represents, not a genuine personal taste for beautiful things, but an artificial passion for rare or expensive things. But a row of books will give a house character and meaning. It will tell you about its owner. It is a window let into the landscape of his life. When I go into a stranger's library I wander round the bookshelves to learn what sort of a person the stranger is, and when he comes in I feel that I know the key to his mind and the range of his interests. A house without books is a mindless and characterless house, no matter how rich the Persian rugs and how elegant the settees and the ornaments. The Persian rugs only tell you that the owner has got money, but the books will tell you whether he has got a mind as well. I was staying not long ago in a Northern town with a man who had a great house and fine grounds, two or three motor-cars, a billiard-room, and a multitude of other luxuries. The only thing he had not got was books. And the effect left on the mind by all his splendours was that he was pauper. "And where are your books?" asked a famous bookman of my acquaintance who was being shown over a West-End palace by the owner, who, in the last twenty years, had made a colossal fortune. "In the City," was the plutocrat's unblushing reply. He gloried in his poverty.

It is not a question of money. I repeat that books are the cheapest as well as the best part of the equipment of a house. You can begin your library with the expenditure of a couple of shillings. Nearly all the best literature in the world is at your command at

Do We Buy Books?

two shillings a volume. For five pounds you can get a library of fifty books which contain "riches fineless." Even if you don't read them yourself, they are a priceless investment for your children. Holmes used to say that it took three generations of sprawling in a library to create a reading man; but I believe that any intelligent child who stumbles upon, let us say, Herodotus or *Two Years Before the Mast* or Prescott's *Conquest of Peru*, or any similar masterpiece, will be caught by the glamour of books and will contract the reading habit for life. And what habit is there to compare with it? What delight is there like the revelation of books, the sudden impact of a master-spirit, the sense of windows flung wide open to the universe? It is these adventures of the mind, the joy of which does not pass away, that give the adventure of life itself beauty and fragrance, and make it

> Rich as the oozy bottom of the deep,
> With sunken wreck and sumless treasuries.

OTHER PEOPLE'S JOBS

I HAVE been following with interest my friend Mr.
Robert Lynd's quest of a soft job in the columns of
The Daily News. I have been following it with interest,
not only because I never willingly miss anything
which that most witty and wise of writers pens, but
also because the subject is near my heart. I say this
without shame. There is nothing discreditable in
desiring an agreeable occupation, light in labour and
heavy in rewards. I do not pretend to have any
passion for work, I know very few people who have,
and I confess that I find most of those few very
undesirable companions. If I were put upon oath
I think I should have to admit that my impulse
to work is the same humble one as Mr. Chesterton
confessed to—

> When I myself perceived that I
> Must work or I should shortly die—

well, then he worked. And when he had driven off
the shadow of death far enough to feel comfortable,
no doubt he left off and did something pleasant. And
so with most of us. It is only our dislike of the undertaker and all that he connotes that sucks us into the
tubes in the morning and spews us out at night, and
keeps us in the interval counting figures, serving out
"sausage and mash," measuring yards of silk, tapping
typewriters, saying "Walk this way, ma'am," trying

Other People's Jobs

boots on other people's feet, shouting "Full up" on buses, and "Stand clear of the gates" in lifts, and a thousand other things that make you tired to think of—things that have to be done, but are not a man's job to do.

Most of our work in this artificial civilisation of ours is like that. The shepherd who keeps sheep on the hillside and the labourer who tills the soil are living a noble life compared with the tawdry little things most of us are condemned to do in cities. We have to do them to keep the undertaker at bay, and we are not to be blamed if we go about with Mr. Lynd looking at other people's jobs and wishing we had got them. Thus he stands in front of the motor show-room, with his face glued to the window, envying the lucky salesman inside, who only has one customer in an hour to attend to, makes a pot of money out of him, and has all the rest of the day in which to smoke and gossip at the door and think about things. In the same way I never pass down Charing Cross Road without pausing in front of the book-shops and thinking what an agreeable time those fellows inside have. Why, my idea of happiness is to leave this tiresome world and go into a library and be forgotten, and here are lucky fellows who have to live in a library to earn their living.

But I daresay it is all an illusion. It is an illusion, no doubt, even in the case of postmen, for whom most of us retain a romantic and indestructible affection. They belong to the earliest of our memories, and get entangled in the clouds of glory, which, according to the poet, we trail into this world with

Other People's Jobs

us from afar. The clouds of glory fade, but the post-man remains as a reminder that we once lived in the Golden Age. Next to the muffin-man, he seemed the most entirely enviable and likeable creature in trousers. The muffin-man, of course, had advantages. There were his muffins to begin with. And there was his bell. To have a bell of your own and to have the privilege of going down any street you liked ringing it as hard as you liked and scattering the good tidings of muffins put a man in a class by himself.

But the postman, if on a lower plane than the muffin-man, had a more continuous joy. He had not a bell of his own, but he had the run of other people's bells. He could ring any bell he liked and bang any knocker as hard as he chose without a thought of running away. And these delights he had every day and several times a day. He could go on ringing bells and knocking at doors till his arm ached. Nobody objected. On the contrary, you looked out for him, hoping that he would come and bang at your door in that breezy way of his. The longer he paused before banging, the better you liked him. It meant—it could only mean—that he had such a lot of letters for you that it took him a long time to find them all.

And, of course, the more letters there were the more joy there must be. That is the miracle with the post-man. He brings bad news and good news and in-different news, but we only remember him by his good news. Like the sun-dial, he only records the sunny hours. He is the hope that springs eternal in the human breast. He comes up the path, probably with a handful of accounts you have not paid, income

Other People's Jobs

tax demands, offers from kind gentlemen to lend you
ten thousand pounds on your note of hand, applica-
tions for subscriptions, and other things that you
would be pleased to do without. But no experience
of the Barmecide feasts he is capable of offering you
affects your faith in him and his good intentions. If
he were to turn back in the middle of the path you
would be disappointed. If he pass by your gate you
are not grateful that he has not brought you ill-news.
You suspect that something pleasant has unaccount-
ably gone astray.

That is as it should be. When we have ceased to
want to hear the postman's knock we may conclude
that we have seen the best of the day, and that the
demon of disillusion has us in thrall. It is to have
given up hope that that legendary ship of our childhood will ever come home. It was that admirable
vessel that made the future such an agreeable prospect. Everything would be possible when our ship
came home. That it was a very rich ship and that it
was on its way we did not doubt, for we had the word
of most responsible people, mothers and aunts and
grandmothers, on the subject. We could not understand why it tarried so long, but we did not suspect
its *bona fides* any more than its seaworthiness. Some
day—it might be any day, possibly even to-morrow—
the postman would come and knock lustily at the
door and bring news that the ship was in port or, at
least, had been sighted from the shore.

And though we have since discovered that those
responsible people were talking less literally than we
thought, and that that magic ship, with its golden

argosy, was a thing of the fancy, we still see the postman turn in at the gate with a mild flutter of expectation. He is himself a sort of ship, laden with mer-
chandise from afar. In his bag there must be incredible
things, and some of them may be for us. It might be
assumed that men whose coming gives so much joy
are themselves joyful, that they love their calling so
much that they would not change with kings, but
experience reveals to us the melancholy truth that
postmen are as afflicted with the discontents of life
as the common run of mortals.

I fancy that if that motor salesman had come to
the door and opened out his mind to Mr. Lynd he
would have told him that selling motors was all
right, but that not selling them, which occupied
about nineteen hours out of twenty, was the most
sickening job under the sun, and that the thing he
really yearned after was to be literary critic, like
that Mr. Robert Lynd, who wrote such stunning
reviews in the papers. Now that *was* a job. There he
sat, in an arm-chair before a ripping fire, surrounded
by all the latest books, with his feet on the mantel-
piece and no reason to put on his boots from morning
to night, reading books and smoking his hardest,
and then taking the author up, as it were, between
thumb and forefinger and showing the world what
an ugly guy of a fellow he was. Fancy being paid to
read books and lamm the writers. Fancy being paid
for having your name in the paper in big type that
anybody could read half a dozen yards away. Yes, that
was the sort of soft job he would like. Motors . . .

That is the way of things. We are all apt to think

Other People's Jobs

we should be happy if we were doing somebody
else's work — the king's, for example. Even the
nursery rhyme inculcates in us the notion that kings
are happy as the day is long, yet no intelligent coal-
heaver who knew the blessings of liberty and obscurity
would be able to endure the boredom and routine
of a calling which compels a man to live as publicly
as a bee in an observation hive. I have known people
even envy a bishop's gaiters, but I should be surprised to learn that there was a single bishop on the
bench who did not wish he could go about in trousers
again, and take up a plain hum-drum occupation in
which he could be as good as he liked without an-
nouncing it about the legs. The truth probably is that
all these dreams of soft jobs are vanity and that the
canker and the worm can gnaw at the heart of the best
of them. I offer this modest reflection to Mr. Lynd in
the hope that he will not cease to write beautiful
articles in order to be an incompetent motor salesman
or to mix drugs in a chemist's shop. I do not think he
is the sort of man who could sell anything, and I fancy
he is just the sort of man who would mix the drugs
more than they ought to be mixed.

WHY I DON'T KNOW

I WAS asked the other day by one of those journals which love vast, resounding themes with which to astonish their readers to write an article on the most important man in the world. I declined, partly because I was busy and partly because I was lazy, but chiefly because I had not a ghost of a notion of the answer. Of course, it would have been possible for me to have discussed the claims of this man and that to pre-eminence, to have contrasted M. Poincaré with Mr. Lloyd George, Mr. Bernard Shaw with Mr. Charlie Chaplin, M. Trotsky with Signor Mussolini, Einstein with Rutherford, and so on; but I should not have answered the question. No one can answer the question. We can all guess; but one thing is pretty certain. We shall all guess wrong. The most important man in the world is somewhere, but he will not be known until he is dead, and we are all dead with him; not until our posterity looks back upon this time and says with one voice, "Behold, the man," as we to-day look back to the great age of Elizabeth and say, "Lo! Shakespeare." No one said it then, and no one thought it. Nearly two centuries had to pass before the true magnitude of this peak became visible and even then it had to be discovered by observers from

Why I Don't Know

afar, by the critics of a foreign land and a foreign tongue.

Was there ever a period in history when the world knew where to look for its chief of men? If ever it might have been expected to pick him out with the certainty of being right it would have been when Augustus Cæsar reigned at Rome over the whole known world. He was so supreme that he seemed less a man than a god. But down in a little province of his vast empire there was a Boy growing up who was destined to change the whole face of the world and to outshine Augustus as the sun outshines a rush-light. The magnificence of Augustus and his empire is an empty memory of nineteen centuries ago, but Christianity is still the mightiest force in the affairs of men.

Or suppose you had been living in the year 1506 in Valladolid, and had asked yourself who was the most important man alive. You would have said the Pope or the Emperor or Ferdinand, without knowing that they were nothing compared with a poor old man who was dying in poverty and neglect in a mean street of that famous city. He did not know himself how vast a thing he had done and how his name would outlive and outsoar those of kings and warriors, poets and statesmen. He did not know that he had not simply found a new way to the East Indies, but had discovered a New World, and that all the vast continent of America would be the everlasting memorial of his life of struggle and disappointment. One would like to think that the spirit of Columbus "poised in the unapparent" has the satisfaction

Why I Don't Know

of knowing what a resounding name he has left behind him.

Let us go on a few years. I will imagine that in 1530 I am asked, not by an editor—for that breed had not then been invented—but by some other curious inquirer, to direct him to the king of men then living. I should probably have answered with some confidence. It was the day of the Great Kings. I suppose three men of such remarkable powers as Henry VIII., Charles V., and Francis I. never reigned in Europe simultaneously. It was only a question of which was the greatest to decide who was the most important man in the world. I daresay I should have decided for Henry; but of course I should have been wrong. The most important man in the world was a person of whom I should not then have heard—a wandering scientist born on the Vistula, Copernicus by name, into whose profound mind there had come the most stupendous conception that ever thrilled the thought of man. The earth was not, as had been supposed through all the ages, the fixed centre of the universe around which the stars moved in obedient subjection, but a little planet rushing with the rest round its great over-lord, the sun. With that terrific discovery, the whole conception of the cosmos was changed, the earth became a speck of dust in the unthinkable vast, religion assumed new meanings, and man fell from his proud pre-eminence as the lord of creation. In its effects it was the most momentous thing that ever happened in the secular history of man; but the point here is that if you and I had been living then and had had Copernicus pointed

Why I Don't Know

out to us in the street we should not have known that he was beyond all comparison the most tremendous figure in the world.

Take another illustration. The end of the eighteenth century was a time of great men. If we had guessed then who was the most important man alive we should have been puzzled to decide between Pitt and Burke, Johnson and Washington, Nelson and Napoleon, and a multitude of others. None of us would have thought of looking for him in the person of a certain gentle, unassuming instrument-maker who filled a modest position in Glasgow University. Yet if the most important man in the world is he who sets in motion the forces—whether of ideas or physical powers—that most profoundly affect the life of men, then no one living from, say, 1760 to 1800, was comparable with James Watt. He inaugurated the Age of Steam. He released the greatest power that the ingenuity of man has ever invented, and the train that thunders through the land, and the ship that ploughs the sea, and the engine that drives a thousand looms are among the prolific children of his genius.

And so I repeat that I do not know who is the most important man in the world. He may be a solitary thinker wrestling with some vast conception that is destined to reshape all our thought. He may be some unknown scientist from whose laboratory there will emerge one day a power that will shake the heavens. He may be a prophet or a teacher who will help us to solve the riddle of this unintelligible world. He may be a discoverer or even a poet. I am sure he will not be a soldier, and I don't think he will be a

Why I Don't Know

politician. These people make a great noise in the the world, but they rarely do anything that matters to posterity. The most important man in the world is probably making no noise at all. His noise will come late like the sound of a great gun heard from afar. But it is a noise that will echo down the ages.

ON ANTI-CLIMAX

THE centenary of the birth of Coventry Patmore
has produced many handsome tributes to that once
popular, but now little-read poet. When I was a boy
The Angel in the House was as familiar as *In Memoriam*,
and Patmore was a more prominent figure in the
literary landscape than Browning. He has long lost
that eminence, but his haughty genius, like that of
Landor, will always command the respectful, if
slightly chilly, admiration of certain minds. "I shall
dine late," said Landor, "but the rooms will be well-
lighted and the company fit, though few."

Patmore, who outlived his earlier reputation, felt
the same assurance about himself. And rightly, for
though it is probable that the dust will be allowed to
gather on the unthumbed *Angel in the House*, some of
his later poems have an energy and nobility that will
keep them alive. *The Farewell*, for example, has the
ring of deathlessness in it as assuredly as Drayton's
Parting, of which it is reminiscent, or Browning's
Last Ride Together. He will not be forgotten, too,
for another reason. Fine poet though he was, he could
come to grief badly, and the stanza with which he
closed his most famous poem will live as an example
of anti-climax:

> But here their converse had its end;
>   For, crossing the Cathedral Lawn,
> There came an ancient college-friend,
>   Who, introduced to Mrs. Vaughan,

On Anti-Climax

Lifted his hat and bowed and smiled,
   And filled her kind large eyes with joy,
By patting on the cheek her child,
   With, "Is he yours, this handsome boy?"

"Who, introduced to Mrs. Vaughan"! Shades of Parnassus! It is easy to see how he came to grief. He had carried his high theme to a close, and wished to end his flight with composed wings and the negligible twitter of the bird at rest. But in the attempt to be simple he stumbled, as much greater poets like Wordsworth have stumbled, on the banal and the commonplace. We suffer from it something of the shock we receive from the historic greeting by Stanley of Livingstone in the depths of the African forest, which is an immortal example of anti-climax. The expedition for the discovery of Livingstone touched the epic note of grand adventure. It held the attention of the world, and the moment of the meeting was charged with the high emotions of a sublime occasion. And when they met (so the record stands), Stanley held out his hand and said, "Dr. Livingstone, I *presume.*" At that artificial word the epic collapses to the dimensions of a suburban reception. It is not easy to imagine what salutation would have fitted the end of so mighty a quest, but if Stanley had said, "Dr. Livingstone, I suppose," or preferably simply the name, the feeling of the occasion would not have been outraged, so slight are the things which separate the sublime from the ridiculous.

A lack of humour as much as of taste is usually the source of the anti-climax, as in the familiar example from the prize poem on the *Mayflower*:

On Anti-Climax

> And so, directed by the hand of God,
> They sailed away until they reached Cape Cod.

The impossible transition from the plane of high spiritual ideas to a mere geographical fact was made grotesque by the name which only a very humourless person could have used in such a connection. Similarly, in the hardly less familiar illustration of bathos:

> Here comes Dalhousie, the great God of War,
> Lieutenant-colonel to the Earl of Mar,

the plunge from the Homeric vein to the Army List could only have been possible to a man who lacked humour even more than the sense of poetry.

That was what was wrong with Alfred Austin, the great master of bathos, who perpetrated more banalities than any poet since Pye. I like best his tribute to the dauntless soldiers:

> They did not know what blench meant,
> So they stayed in their entrenchment.

Here the grotesqueness of the rhyme emphasises the absurdity of the illustration. It is not staying in an entrenchment, but leaving an entrenchment that requires courage. Like the much greater Patmore, Austin could collapse into the commonplace in trying to achieve the simple and artless, as when he wrote:

> The spring time, O, the spring time,
>   Who does not know it well—
> When the little birds begin to sing
> And the buds begin to swell.

Contrast these tinkling syllables with the surge of

emotion with which another poet could charge the song of the birds and the bloom of the flowers:

> Ye flowery banks o' bonnie Doon,
> How can ye blume sae fair?
> How can ye chant, ye little birds,
> And I sae fu' o' care?

I suppose no poet was ever more royally regardless of the smaller niceties of the poet's craft than Burns was, but it would not be easy to find in all his work a case where he comes down with the broken wing of anti-climax.

THE UNKNOWN WARRIOR [1]

WE shall not know his name. It will never be known, and we should not seek to know it. For in that nameless figure that is borne over land and sea to mingle its dust with the most sacred dust of England, we salute the invisible hosts of the fallen. We do not ask his name or whence he comes. His name is legion and he comes from a hundred fields, stricken with a million deaths.

Gaily or sadly, he went out to battle. We see him, as in a vision, streaming in by a thousand roads, down from the Hebrides and the glens of the North, from the mines of Durham and the shipyards of the Clyde and Tyne and the bogs of Ireland, out of the factories of Lancashire and Yorkshire, up from the pastures of East Anglia and the moors of Devon, over the seas from distant lands, whither he had gone to live his life and whence he returns at the call of a duty that transcends life. In his speech we hear the echoes of a hundred countrysides, from the strong burr of Aberdeen to the lilt of Dorset and the broad-vowelled speech of Devon; but whatever the accent it mingles in that song about Tipperary which, by the strangest of ironies, lives in the mind with the sound of the tramp of millions to battle.

[1] Written on the day of the interment of the Unknown Warrior in Westminster Abbey.

The Unknown Warrior

He takes a thousand shapes in our minds. We see him leaving the thatched cottage in some remote village, his widowed mother standing at the doorway and shading her eyes to catch the last glimpse of him as he turns into the high-road that shuts him from her sight; we see him throwing aside his books and bounding out of school or college with the light of adventure in his eye; we see him closing his little shop, laying aside his pen, putting down mallet and chisel, hammer and axe. We see him taking a million pitiful farewells, his young wife hanging about his neck in an agony of grief, his little children weeping for they know not what, with that dread foreboding that is the affliction of childhood, the old people standing by with a sorrow that has passed beyond the relief of tears. Here he is the lover and there the son and there the husband and there the brother, but everywhere he is the sacrifice. While others remain behind, perhaps to win ignoble riches and rewards, he goes out to live in mud and filth and die a lonely and horrible death far from his home and all that he loved.

And he is chosen, not because he is the tainted wether of the flock, meetest for sacrifice, but because he is the pride of the flock. In him we see the youth of England, all that is bravest and best and richest in promise, brains that could have won the priceless victories of peace, sinews that could have borne the burden of labour, singers and poets and statesmen in the green leaf, the Rupert Brookes, the Raymond Asquiths, the Gladstones, the Keelings, the finest flower of every household, all offered as a sacrifice on the insane and monstrous altar of war.

The Unknown Warrior

And with the mind's eye we follow him as he is
swallowed up in the furnace. We see him falling on
that desperate day at Suvla Bay, perishing in the
deserts of Mesopotamia, struck down in the snow-
storm on Vimy Ridge, dying on the hundred battle-
fields of the Somme, disappearing in the sea of mud
churned up at Passchendaele, falling like autumn
leaves in the deadly salient of Ypres, stricken in those
unforgettable days of March, when the Fifth Army
broke before the German onset. His bones lie scattered
over a thousand alien fields from the Euphrates to
the Scheldt and lie on the floor of every wandering
sea. From the Somme to Zeebrugge his cemeteries
litter the landscape, and in those graves lie the youth
of England and the hearts of those who mourn.

Now one comes back, the symbol of all who have
died and who will never return. He comes, unknown
and unnamed, to take his place among the illustrious
dead. And it is no extravagant fancy to conceive the
spirits of that great company, the Chathams and
Drydens and Johnsons, poets, statesmen and warriors,
receiving him into their midst in the solemn Abbey
as something greater and more significant than they.
For in him they will see the emblem of the mightiest
tribute ever laid on the nation's altar. In him we do
reverence to that generation of Britain's young men-
hood that perished in the world's madness and sleeps
for ever in foreign lands.

None of us will look on that moving scene without
emotion. But something more will be required of us
than a spasm of easy, tearful emotion that exhausts
itself in being felt. What have we, the living, to say

The Unknown Warrior

to the dead who pass by in shadowy hosts? They died for no mean thing. They died that the world might be a better and a cleaner place for those who lived and for those who come after. As that unknown soldier is borne down Whitehall he will issue a silent challenge to the living world to say whether it was worthy of his sacrifice. And if we are honest with ourselves we shall not find the answer easy.

NAMING THE BABY

I TAKE no responsibility in the matter. It is true that I was consulted, but only in a sort of Elder Statesman capacity. I happened to be the grandfather in the case, and my opinion was asked, not as having any artistic merit, but as a tribute to my ancestral status. Moreover, I was to be the godfather, and could not be decently left out of the discussion.

At this stage the current was running strong in favour of "Martin."

"Why Martin?" I asked. "There has never been a Martin in the family, and the only Martins I can recall are Martin Luther and Martin Tupper. But why commemorate them?"

"We aren't proposing to commemorate them. We are not thinking of them. We are thinking of Martin on its merits. There's a nice clean, sharp quality about it. It's not too unusual, and just unusual enough —plain and not too plain. It has distinction without frills. That's the case for Martin."

"But if you want a name with that sort of flavour," said I, "why not Crispin?"

"Crispin, by Jove! That's an idea. Why, Sylvia, why didn't you think of Crispin? Of course, it's Crispin. It fits him like a glove. Here, pass Crispin over to me. What clarity! What austerity! What a flavour of the antique world! Henry the Fifth before

Naming the Baby

Agincourt, and all the rest of it. It's like a beautiful frosty morning—sunshine and a nip in the air, a clean wind and a clear sky."

But when at the next conference the subject was resumed, Crispin had passed under a cloud. It was a little too chill—a little too much of autumn about it. And it called attention to itself. Now Philip—that had the smack of high summer. It was round and full and came trippingly from the tongue. And as for its traditions, these were abundant, Philip of Macedon and Philip Sidney.

"And Philip the Second," I said.

"Well, we must take the good with the bad. And after all the name's the thing."

"Have you thought of Christopher?"

"Yes, for one whole evening Christopher went like a gale of wind. I forget why we dropped it. Why did we drop it, Sylvia? There must have been some reason, but I can't for the life of me think what it was or what it could be. Christopher. . . . Yes, I think we shall have to reconsider Christopher, Sylvia."

That evening there was a ring on the telephone. "It's all right," said the voice. "We've had a brain-wave. We've decided on Antony—A-n-t-o-n-y—no 'h' of course."

"You mean the sinner, not the saint. I don't like Mark Antony. Can't forgive him that affair of Cicero's head."

"Well, they all used to do things like that in those days."

"But why allude to the fellow?"

"We are not alluding to him."

Naming the Baby

"You can't help alluding to him. It's the greatest one-man name in the world. Why not go for simplicity? There's John. Glorious name, John—fits anybody—splendid traditions, John Milton, John Dryden, John Bright, John Bunyan, John Donne——"

"Then you don't like Antony."

"I don't say that. I said I didn't like Mark Antony."

When the jury met again, however, Antony, like Philip and Christopher, was out of the running, and Martin had reappeared. There was such a quietude about Martin, you know. It was calm, it was self-controlled, it was full of peace, and yet it wasn't dull. There couldn't possibly be anything wrong with a fellow named Martin.

"Well," said I, "Martin Luther kicked up a tolerable dust in the world, and Martin Tupper was as dull as an oyster. Now Stephen——"

"Yes, Stephen is a fine name. We've thought a lot about Stephen. It has just the right note of romance without being romantic. I think we turned it down because we thought it was rather 'defeatist' in spirit. There was Stephen who was stoned—wasn't he?—and King Stephen who lost his crown—didn't he?—and Uncle Stephen who was drowned, and things like that. We don't want to start the boy with a 'defeatist' name. But Stephen is beautiful, I think we shall have to think about Stephen again, Sylvia."

And they did. "We've settled on Stephen," was the eleventh-hour bulletin from headquarters.

I was a little late when I reached the church, and the christening group was already around the font with the clergyman in attendance. The service

Naming the Baby

proceeded at once, and reached the point at which the clergyman demanded the name of "this child."

"Michael," came the astonishing reply.

I looked up and caught a mischievous glint in the maternal eye. "Well, you see," she said afterwards, "we were quite exhausted with the search, and fell on Michael in desperation. And he *was* born on St. Michael's Day. And there was Michael Angelo, you know. Anyhow, it's done now, and can't be undone. But I do hope Michael——"

"Mike," I said.

"No, no, it's to be Michael—I do hope Michael will like it."

. . . . . .

"How's Michael?" I asked a few days later when the father visited me.

"The baby is going on splendidly," he said.

"'The baby,'" I said. "Why not Michael?"

"Oh, something's got to be done. We can never leave the poor child with that name tied to him. We think of calling him Martin."

"Or Stephen," I said.

THE CULT OF THE KNIFE AND FORK

I was walking in the Chiltern Hills with a friend not long ago when we turned into the inn at Chenies for lunch. There were only two people in the dining-room—a man and, I take it, his wife, who were sitting at a table laden with a cold roast of beef, vegetables, pickles, cheese and bread, and large tankards of beer. The man was a hefty person with red hair, a red face, and a "fair round belly." He took no notice of our entrance, and he took no notice of the timid little woman in front of him. He gave his undivided attention to his knife and fork and the joint before him. He cut and came again with the steady gravity of a man who took his victuals seriously and had no time for frivolous talk. When at last the fury of his appetite abated, he took a last deep draught from the tankard, drew his napkin across his mouth, stretched himself, and, speaking for the first time to the timid little woman in front of him, said:

"Well, we'd better be getting on if we're going to catch that train to Rickmansworth" (two stations or so off).

"But what do we want to stop at Rickmansworth for?" ventured the timid little woman.

"What do we want to stop at Rickmansworth for?" repeated the man in a tone in which astonishment and

The Cult of the Knife and Fork

indignation struggled for mastery. *"Well, I suppose we've got to have tea!"*

He spoke as though the deepest feelings of his nature had been wounded. He was having a day's outing in the country, and here was this insensible woman before him who actually wanted to know what they were going to Rickmansworth for. What had they come out for if it was not to have lunch at Chenies *and* tea at Rickmansworth? In his mind Chenies lived as a place where you got lashings of cold beef and pickles, washed down with good ale, at the inn, and Rickmansworth as a place where you called to have tea and eggs and bread and butter and jam. I do not speak disrespectfully of those to whom the memory of good food hangs like a halo round a place. Hazlitt remembered Llangollen, not merely because he first read the *New Eloise* there, but because he read it to the accompaniment of a bottle of sherry and a cold chicken. And again: "I remember the leg of Welsh mutton and the turnips that day had the finest flavour imaginable," he says, when referring to his first meeting with Coleridge.

Indeed, not the least of Hazlitt's charms is his hearty delight in the table. His adventures have a trick of ending in the cheerful music of knife and fork. Thus he tells how in his youthful days when he was trying to live by art he painted a portrait of a Manchester manufacturer, and being very hungry, having lived for the past fortnight chiefly on coffee, he slurred over the painting of his sitter's coat in order that he might hear the five guineas reward jingling in his pocket. Then, the guineas secure, he hurried to the market-place and dined on sausages and mashed potatoes, "a noble dish for strong stomachs; and while they were getting ready and I could hear them hissing in the pan, I read a volume of *Gil Blas* containing the account of the fair Aurora."

But with all the gusto of these and many similar allusions to food, it will be observed that the pleasures of eating were incidental and not primary. It was the associations of the food that made it memorable. The sherry and the chicken, like Llangollen itself, were irradiated by the spirit of Rousseau, and the Welsh mutton and the turnips lingered on the palate of memory with the impression of Coleridge's astonishing eloquence. It was the intellectual zest of the occasion that added a touch of poetry to the food. The Welsh mutton caught the rapture of the prophet, the sherry glowed with the fire of new thought and the hissing of the sausages and mash in the pan was mingled with the tale of the fair Aurora. That is the way to dignify the remembrance of our creature comforts. It is no dishonour even to the Finsteraarhorn to remember the noble bowl of steaming hot soup that you had in the hut when the climb was done, and many a fine walk is rounded off in retrospect by the fare that awaited us at the inn. Even bread and cheese and beer may be suffused with the glory of a great adventure and Mr. George Saintsbury, who has as much zest over his food as Hazlitt had, will grow lyrical even over sandwiches, taken to the right accompaniment of time and place.

But to remember Chenies for its beef and pickles is to exalt beef and pickles to too high a place in our affections. I have known men who have travelled much and who seem to have brought nothing back from their travels but menu cards. Such a one was coming up the other day from Devonshire, whither he had been for a holiday. I know no finer country for a holiday, nor one better worth growing dithyrambic about. After much travelling and many affairs of the heart with the English counties I think my verdict has gone finally to Devonshire. Where shall we find such colour, such moorlands, such a variety of coast-line, so warm and generous a feeling about Nature and man? If I had a second innings on earth and had my choice of birthplace I think I should choose to be born a Devon man. So I think would that man in the railway-carriage, but for other reasons than mine. He was an amiable and gossipy man who babbled to the company about his holiday experiences. He had been to many places on the South Devon coast, but so far as one could gather he had been eating all the time. Every place recalled some meal. There was Dartmouth, for example. If you ever went to Dartmouth be sure to go to such-and-such a tea-shop. Top-hole it was. Best place for tea in the town. You could have what they called "a light tea," and a very nice tea it was, with home-made jam and Devonshire cream. His face glowed with the succulent thought. *Or* you could have a heavy tea, a sort of a high tea, the constituents of which he recited with great precision, as a man might particularise his strokes at golf or his hands at cards or the mountains he had climbed.

Then there was Teignmouth. He went there and

The Cult of the Knife and Fork

it was a fine place. And if you ever went to Teignmouth he had one piece of advice to give. Don't miss having lunch at the "Boar's Head" or some such place. No end of a lunch. And reasonable too. Not cheap, mind you. He was not a person who believed in cheapness. But the quality! And with this introduction he travelled over the menu, the record of which occupied quite a substantial part of the journey to London. After this he continued the itinerary of his travels in quest of meals. He went up the Teign to Newton Abbot, and there or thereabouts he struck a most wonderful cockle tea. The cockles, it seemed, came out of the river, and it was his solid conviction that Newton Abbot was a place very well worth visiting if it was only to know what cockles could be like when they came fresh out of the water, and were taken to the accompaniment of the right sort of tea.

And so be babbled on about the places he had been to and the food he had eaten in them until one might have thought that Devonshire was a land strewn with tea-shops and restaurants. I offer him as a cautionary tale for those who take the cult of the knife and fork a thought too seriously.

A SOLILOQUY IN A GARDEN

I SPENT this morning hoeing in a part of the garden which had run to weeds very miserably. Thistles, nettles, chickweed, and a multitude of other undesirable growths had taken possession and extinguished every decent inhabitant of the soil. There are few more depressing spectacles than a garden that has fallen on evil times and has become a sort of slum of nature, where everything that is beautiful and wholesome has been trampled out of existence and everything that is coarse and worthless riots in profusion and triumph. As I hoed the weeds up I indulged in the familiar reflection on the prodigality with which Nature looks after the weeds and the parsimony she shows for the more delicate and beautiful of her children. Lincoln said that God must love the common people, or He would not have made so many of them. Nature must love the weeds, or she would not have made them such sturdy fellows and given them such a lusty hold on life.

For the truth is that in the battlefield of the garden barbarism is never suppressed. All the cunning of the gardener is needed to keep it in reasonable check. Let the watchman sleep but a week and the barbarian hosts will have begun to overrun the civilised population that his labour and science have planted and nurtured. Let him sleep for a month and the work of a season will be undone. The strawberry bed will be a ruin, the vegetable garden will be yellow with charlock and creeping buttercup, and white with sheep's parsley, and scarlet with poppies, and the flower-beds will be a forlorn picture of rank growths. It is a familiar saying of the gardener that one year's seeds means ten years' weeds, and it is certainly a slow business to redeem soil that has once lapsed into foulness.

This train of thought took a wider circle as I proceeded with my task. The garden became a symbol that seemed to offer a not inapposite comment on the problem that is disturbing so many minds at this time. Mankind has for some years made so shocking an exhibition of itself that there seems nothing to be said in our defence. On the face of it, the argument is with the Dean Inges who regard the human growth as incurably bad and progress as an idle illusion. We just go round and round in circles. Sometimes we seem to be getting our garden of life civilised and cultivated. At last, we say, we have got the weeds under. Then suddenly we relapse into barbarism and all our delicate cultures vanish before the onrush of the blind furies and savageries that may be chained in us, but are never extinguished. It is a depressing philosophy, and in the light of our recent experience it would not be easy to entertain the dream of human perfectibility which was so popular an idea with the philosophic Radical of a century ago. It would hardly be possible to claim that human nature is better than it was a thousand or perhaps ten thousand years ago. Our garden is as

A Soliloquy in a Garden

full of potential weeds as ever it was, and when they spring up they are as obscene and devastating as ever they were.

If that were all we might despair. But it is not less true that the gardening has not been in vain. Even in the presence of the terrific reaction of these days it is possible to maintain that human society has won great victories over the weeds of human nature. Man may not be better than he was ten thousand years ago, but the community of men is better. The laws under which we live are humaner laws than ever obtained in the past. There is more equity and justice in our common relations, more respect for human life, more sense of human rights and liberties. We make war savagely, but we do not massacre the women and children, and we do not enslave the defeated as the Greeks did.

Contrast the position of women in the modern world with their position in the Tudor world, or the treatment of children to-day with their treatment in the not far distant days when Elizabeth Barrett Browning wrote *The Cry of the Children*, and we have a measure of real progress. When Dr. Clifford was once interrupted by a "voice" which denied that the world was growing better, he replied: "But I know it is growing better. I know that when I was a child of eight, I was called at five o'clock in the morning to go to work in a factory for twelve hours a day, and I know that to-morrow morning there will not be a child in all the land who will suffer that wrong." Or to apply another test. Turn to Plutarch's *Lives* and count the violent deaths that befell his subjects.

A Soliloquy in a Garden

I doubt whether one in four died a natural death. To be famous in the ancient world was to be doomed. But there is little personal peril in being either famous or infamous in these days.

And so I think the case is not quite so black as our pessimists paint it. We shall never subdue the old Adam that dwells in us, but we have collectively developed a social conscience which does keep him in check. The gardening is not profitless. The weeds are always lurking in the soil ready to spring up and turn the garden to a desolation, just as the germs of pneumonia are said to be in every nostril waiting for the moment of weakness in the body to leap to the attack. The moral to be drawn from these desperate times is not the futility of weeding, but the urgency of it. We can easily be too despairing about ourselves. Perhaps after all we are only in the infancy of our days, and though as men and women we may never achieve perfectibility we need not despair of strengthening our social defences against future collapses into barbarism. Human nature may be as bad as it seems, but it is still possible to say with Arnold that there is a stream of tendency in us that makes for righteousness. So let us get on with our weeding.

A NIGHT'S LODGING

I AWOKE this morning with the sort of feeling a healthy child awakes with on Christmas Day. That is to say, I awoke with delight at the idea of getting up. I was in a strange bed in a strange city. I had arrived in the strange city late overnight, and had had to take what lodging I could find. Until I lay down in my bed I had no idea how uncomfortable a bed could be. It was as cold as charity and as hard as a tax-gatherer. The bolster was the shape of a large round sausage, and the pillow was the shape of a sausage also. They were a relentless pair of ruffians, cold-hearted, passionless brutes, stolid and unresponsive, deaf alike to appeal or rebuke. I coaxed them with the flat of my hand, and they scowled unmoved; I smote them with my closed fist, and they took no more notice of it than if their name had been Dempsey.

I did not know that I could hate any inanimate thing so much as I hated that pillow and that bolster. I did not know that such oceans of blind anger were bottled up within me. I banged them against each other with savage joy. I threw them on the floor and danced and stamped on them. I knelt on them; I sat on them; finally I kicked them, not in the hope of doing them any good (hope had by this time died within me), but for the simple delight of kicking the abominations.

Then, warmed with these various exercises, I put

A Night's Lodging

the things back and got into bed. It was as I expected. The mattress was a fit companion for the pillow and bolster. It lay like a newly ploughed field, every furrow deeply graven, every ridge with the edge of a dulled razor. It was not a field of warm loam or generous greensand that yielded to the touch. It was a field of stubborn Essex clay, cold and dank and merciless. The expanse was enormous. It seemed that during that measureless night I travelled miles to and fro across the field in search of a furrow into which I could wedge myself. I tried it on the east side, and I tried it on the west, and I tried it all between. I tried it longitudinally; I tried it latitudinally; I tried it diagonally. The way with a bed like this, I said to myself, is not to get in the furrows, but to lie across the ridges. But when I did that I felt like a toad under the harrow, when "ilka tooth gies him a tig," and I resumed my search for a furrow that would give me a welcome.

In the intervals I slept and had wild dreams in which I met Apollyon straddling across my path. He came at me with fire belching from his nostrils, but I gave him a mighty thwack with a bolster I happened to be carrying, and he fell with an awful thud and split his head open on a ridge of the ploughed field where the combat occurred. I daresay I slept more than I imagined, for I share Lord Granville's view on the subject. Believing that he was a victim of insomnia, he took a house in Carlton House Terrace, within sound of Big Ben, and was comforted to find that, in spite of nights which seemed to pass without a wink of sleep, he only heard the great bell once or twice.

A Night's Lodging

I did not do so well as that. As I fought with the furrows I heard all the night sounds of the strange city without—the ringing of tram bells, the jolting of wagons, the songs of revellers, and so on—die down until all was quiet. I dozed and wakened and wakened and dozed, praying for the dawn as fervently as ever Wellington prayed for Blücher. Once I dreamed that I had gone into Hell, and heard the cries of the souls in torment, and waking I found that the strange city without was coming to life again with a jangle of hoots and whistles and screams. Perhaps, I felt, my dream was not very far wrong. I lay and listened to the mad chorus. I had never imagined that there could be so many whistles whistling with such different notes, high notes and low notes, clear notes and foggy notes, shrieking and growling like a whole menagerie of wild beasts hungering for blood. Intermittent noises began to be heard in the corridor. People were moving about. There was a swishing sound from the next room. A church clock outside began to strike, and I counted the strokes as a miser counts his money—one, two three, four, five, six, SEVEN. It seemed too good to be true. I punched the pillow to make certain I was awake, and, under the comfortable assurance that release was at hand, fell to sleep again in my furrowed field. When I woke next, the room was light. I leapt from bed and kicked the pillow joyfully across the room. But the bolster I subjected to no such indignity. After all, it had done me a good turn with Apollyon, and I called the account square.

Two hours later I am in the train fleeing from the

A Night's Lodging

strange city. I had never been to it before, and I daresay I shall never go to it again. But I shall always remember it as the City of Dreadful Night. I feel now that I, too, have been with Æneas into Hell. Perhaps it is unfair to the strange city. I daresay love and peace and beauty dwell there as abundantly as in most places. But I am content to leave the discovery of them to others.

THOSE PEOPLE NEXT DOOR

THE case which has occupied the courts recently of the man who beat a tin can as a way of retaliating upon a neighbour who strummed the piano touches one of the most difficult problems of urban life. We who live in the cities all have neighbours, and for the most part "thin partitions do our realms divide." It is true that, however thin the walls, we seldom know our neighbours. If the man who has lived next door to me in a northern suburb for the last half-dozen years stopped me in the Strand or came and sat down beside me in a restaurant I should not, as the saying is, know him from Adam. In this vast whirlpool of London he goes his way and I go mine, and I daresay our paths will not cross though we go on living beside each other until one or other of us takes up a more permanent abode.

I do not know whether he is short or tall, old or young, or anything about him, and I daresay he is in the same state of contented ignorance about me. I hear him when he pokes the fire on his side late at night, and I suppose he hears me when I poke the fire on my side. Our intercourse is limited to the respective noises we make with the fire-irons, the piano, and so on. When he has friends to visit him we learn something about him from the sounds they make, the music they affect, and the time they go

Those People Next Door

away (often unconscionably late). But apart from that vague intimation, my neighbour might be living in Mars and I might be living in Sirius, for all we know, or care, about each other. Perhaps some day his house (or mine) will be on fire, and then I daresay we shall become acquainted. But apart from some such catastrophe as this there seems no reason why we should ever exchange a word on this side of the grave.

It is not pride or incivility on either side that keeps us remote from each other. It is simply our London way. People are so plentiful that they lose their identity. By the Whitestone Pond at Hampstead not long ago I met my old friend John O'Connor—"Long John," as he was affectionately called in the House of Commons, of which he was for so long one of the most popular members—and he said, in reply to inquiries, that he was living in Frognal, had lived there for years, "next door to Robertson Nicoll—not that I should know him," he added, "for I don't think I have ever set eyes on him." And I should have expected to find that Sir William was no better informed about his neighbour than his neighbour was about him. In London men are as lonely as oysters, each living in his own shell. We go out into the country to find neighbours. If the man next door took a cottage a mile away from me in the country I should probably know all about him, his affairs, his family, his calling, and his habits inside a week, and be intimate enough with him in a fortnight to borrow his garden-shears or his bill-hook. This is not always so idyllic as it seems. Village life can be poisoned by neighbours until the

Those People Next Door

victim pines for the solitude of a London street, where neighbours are so plentiful that you are no more conscious of their individual existence than if they were blackberries on a hedgerow.

On the occasions on which we become acutely conscious of our neighbours, the temptation is to think ill of them. For example, we were all late the other morning, and Matilda, whose function it is to keep us up to time, explained that she had overslept herself because of those people next door. Four o'clock it was, m'm, before the din ended. Some of us had lost count of the hours at two and others at three but Matilda was emphatic. She had heard the last of the revellers go away in a car, and had looked at her watch and it was exactly four. No one disputed her word. It was gratifying to know that the hour was four rather than three. If it had been five we should doubtless have been still more gratified. It would have made the case against those people next door still blacker. And it can never be too black for their deserts. Our neighbours are at once too near to us and too far away from us. If they were under our own roof we might be able to make something of them; if they were only in the next street we could forget all about them. But they are just far enough away to escape our celestial influence and quite close enough to be a nuisance.

They are always in the wrong. Consider the hours they keep — entirely different from our hours and therefore entirely reprehensible. If they do not offend by their extravagant piety they shock you by their levity. Perhaps they play tennis on Sunday, or perhaps

Those People Next Door

they don't, and in either case they are vulnerable to criticism. They always manage to be gay when you are sleepy. They take a delight in going away for more holidays than you can possibly have, or perhaps they don't go away for holidays at all, in which case their inferiority is clearly established. If they are not guilty of criminal waste, they can be convicted of shabby parsimony. They either dress too luxuriously or do not dress luxuriously enough for the decencies of the neighbourhood. We suspect that they are no better than they should be. Observe the frequency with which their servants come and go. Depend upon it, they find those people next door impossible. Their habits and their friends, the music they play, the pets that they keep, the politics they affect, the newspapers they read—all these things confirm our darkest fears.

It is possible to believe anything about them—especially the worst. What are those strange sounds that penetrate the wall in the small hours? Surely that is the chink of coin! And those sudden shrieks and gusts of laughter? Is there not an alcoholic suggestion about such undisciplined hilarity? We know too much about them, and do not know enough. They are revealed to us in fragments, and in putting the fragments together we do not spare them. There is nothing so misleading as half heard and half-understood scraps. And the curious thing about those people next door is that, if you ever come to know them, you find they are not a bit like what you thought they were. You find to your astonishment that they have redeeming features. Perhaps they find that we have redeeming features too. For the chastening truth is that we all play the rôle of those people next door to somebody. We are all being judged, and generally very unfavourably judged, on evidence which, if we knew it, would greatly astonish us. It might help us to be a little more charitable about those people next door if we occasionally remembered that we are those people next door ourselves.

But the St. John's Wood case illustrates the frail terms on which immunity from annoyance by neighbours is enjoyed. Two musicians dwelling in one house gave lessons to pupils on the piano, and the man next door, who objected to his peace being disturbed in this way, took his revenge by banging on tin cans, and otherwise making things unpleasant for the musicians. I do not know what the law said on the subject. It may be admitted that the annoyances were equal in effect, but they were not the same in motive. In the one case the motive was the reasonable one of earning an honest living: there was no deliberate intention of being offensive to the neighbours. In the other case, the motive was admittedly to make a demonstration against the neighbours. What is to be done in such circumstances? It is not an offence to play the piano in one's own house even for a living. On the other hand, it is hard, especially if you don't like music, or perhaps even more if you do, to hear the scales going on the piano next door all day.

The question of motive does not seem to be relevant. If my neighbour makes noises which render my life intolerable, it is no answer to say that he makes them for a living and without intending to

Those People Next Door

destroy my peace. He does destroy my peace, and it is no comfort to be assured that he does not mean to. Hazlitt insisted that a man might play the trombone in his own house all day if he took reasonable measures to limit the annoyance to his neighbours; but Hazlitt had probably never lived beside a trombone. I find the argument is leading me on to the side of the tin-can gentleman, and I don't want it to do that, for my sympathies are with the musicians. And yet——

Well, let us avoid a definite conclusion altogether and leave the incident to make us generally a little more sensitive about the feelings of our neighbours. They cannot expect us never to play the piano, never to sit up late, never to be a little hilarious, any more than we can expect never to be disturbed by them. But the amenities of neighbourliness require that we should mutually avoid being a nuisance to each other as much as we can. And if our calling compels us to be a little noisy, we should bear that in mind when we choose a house and when we choose the room in which we make our noises. The perfect neighbour is one whom we never see and whom we never hear except when he pokes the fire.

HOW WE SPEND OUR TIME

I READ an entertaining article in the *Observer* the other Sunday, which set me to the unusual task of making a calculation. Figures are not my strong point, and sums I abhor. But this article launched me on the unfamiliar task of making a sum. I hope I have done it correctly, but any schoolboy who cares to audit the account will be able to convict me if I am wrong. The article was the record of a gentleman who had, in the course of the past twelve years, played twenty thousand rubbers of auction bridge, and had kept a careful account of his experiences, the proportions of games he had won and lost, the average of "hundred aces" and "yarboroughs" he had had, how he had fared with "honours," with many curious points which had arisen, and which were no doubt illuminating to the student of the game.

But it was not these things which set me adding, subtracting, multiplying and dividing. My knowledge of bridge is as contemptible as my handicap at golf. The author of the article would not sit down at the same table, probably not in the same room, with such a 'prentice hand as I am at the game. Nor was it the financial aspect of the matter that interested me. That side of the story was not without its attractions. The player, on the analysis of his own and his opponents' "hands" over the twelve years showed, had had distinctly the worse of the luck, but he was obviously a good player, for he had won at fifty-five per cent. of his sittings and, playing generally for half-crown rubbers, had won in the twelve years £2750 of the £5000 that had changed hands in the games, each year having shown a profit on his labours.

There was, however, one item which was missing from this elaborate stocktaking, and it was this item that started my sum. I began to be interested in this gentleman from the point of view of the time he had devoted to the game over a period of years, which had not been without their anxieties. This consideration touched a wider question about which I have often thought vaguely and idly—the question, that is, of how the average man passes his time. Here was an average man of a certain class who had incidentally given me a hint to build up his time-sheet form. Taking an hour as the average time occupied by a rubber — which, with intervals and interruptions, seems a moderate estimate—I found that during the twelve years he had spent twenty thousand hours at the card-table—that is, two years and rather more than three months, day and night.

That was a substantial chunk of the twelve years to start with. I came next to the item of sleep, and assuming that, having made up his nightly account of the day's play, our author indulged in the normal eight hours of repose, I found that in the twelve years he had accounted for 34,840 hours in this way, and my schoolboy will, I hope, agree with me that this amounts in sum to approximately four years of sleep, day and night. I came next to meals. A man who can spend five hours a day at cards as an amusement will, I am sure, not hurry over his meals. He will take his lunch at his club, and his coffee and gossip after lunch, and he will dine well and leisurely before turning to the solid work of the card-table, for no doubt most of his card-playing will be done after dinner. Three hours a day is a reasonable allowance for the meal intervals, which, on this basis, account for 12,140 hours, or one year and three-eighths, during the twelve years. Holidays and Sundays (with due deduction on items already accounted for, cards, sleep, meals) account for a further half-year over the twelve years. For all the odds and ends of things, the outdoor recreations, golf, motoring, the daily journeys to and from town, theatres, visits to church, the occasional day at Lord's, the reading of newspapers, parties, public meetings, novel-reading, and so on, an average of two hours a day must be allowed, giving 8760 hours in the twelve years, or, roughly, a year of time. These items make up 75,680 hours out of the 105,120 hours into which the twelve years are divided. There remain 25,060 hours, or two years and seven-eighths, which I will charitably assume are devoted to work. On this basis my sum is as follows:

Sleep	4 years
Work	$2\frac{7}{8}$ years
Cards	$2\frac{1}{3}$ years
Meals	$1\frac{3}{8}$ years
Odds and ends . . .	1 year
Holidays	$\frac{1}{2}$ year
Approximately . .	12 years

How We Spend Our Time

I present the result to the *Observer* gentleman as a footnote to his entertaining article. Far be it from me to moralise about it. If the misuse of time were a hanging matter, few of us would escape the scaffold. I daresay I have wasted as much time in the twelve years as our bridge-player has done, though in different ways. But I think he will agree that the sum is worth doing and worth thinking about, and that when next he says that he has not time for this, that, or the other, he will know he is not telling the truth.

And while he is thinking about it, I will venture to recall for him an old story which he may have heard, but which is worth telling on the chance that he has not. Herbert Spencer was once staying at an hotel and, being fond of billiards, strolled into the billiard-room where he saw a young man who invited him to play a game. Spencer agreed and "broke," unfortunately leaving his ball on the baulk line, but playable. It was in the days when the "feather" stroke was allowed (I fancy it is now barred) and the young man took his cue and ran out by means of that delicate device. When he had reached his "100," the philosopher, putting up his cue with which he had not scored a point, addressed him thus: "A certain degree of facility in games of skill is a pleasant and desirable accomplishment; but, young man, such facility as you have displayed this evening is evidence of a misspent youth."

A SENTENCE OF DEATH

"THE most dramatic thing I remember? I need not pause to answer that question," said my companion. "Do you recall the Lipski case? Ah, well, you will know what a sensation it created. It occurred in the hey-day of the great Stead at the *Pall Mall*. What a flair the fellow had for a sensation, and what a frenzy he could communicate to the public mind. Lipski had been sentenced to death for the murder of his paramour, and doubtless would have been hanged quite quietly but for the fact that Stead became interested in the case and convinced that the man was innocent. There was enough ground for the belief to warrant what would now be called a 'stunt,' and Stead seized his opportunity in his own incomparable fashion, and a raging, tearing propaganda followed in the Press. The public mind was lashed into a fury of indignation. Petitions poured in for the reprieve of the condemned man; demonstrations took place in the streets; crowds assembled in front of Buckingham Palace to wring the Royal prerogative out of the Queen.

"Day succeeded day, and still the storm rose, and still the Home Secretary held his hand. The right of criminal appeal did not exist in those days, and Henry Matthews, the Home Secretary, had no guidance to rely on except that of the judge who had tried the

A Sentence of Death

case, Fitzjames Stephen, and Stephen would commit himself to neither 'yea' nor 'nay,' but took refuge behind the jury's verdict, and left the matter there. The Home Secretary was in despair. Daily he saw himself held up to execration as a murderer, daily the petitions poured in, and the crowds gathered in the streets.

"Saturday came, and on Monday the execution was to take place. Appeals to Stephen were in vain, and every detail of the evidence had been examined again and again without a ray of new light. It was not only the condemned man whose fate was involved. If he was guilty and Matthews reprieved him, the latter would have yielded to an ignorant clamour and disgraced his office; if he was not guilty, and Matthews did not reprieve him, he would have executed an innocent man in the face of an unprecedented public warning. The day passed in anxious and ceaseless inquiry. In the afternoon he sent word to Stephen. He must see him once more. They could meet at the Home Office the following (Sunday) evening at five o'clock.

"I was then on the Home Office staff, and it was my duty to be in attendance while this critical conference was in progress. Time passed without a sound or sign coming from the room where the argument of life or death was proceeding. In the quiet of the late Sunday afternoon the chimes of Big Ben sounded the quarters from the Clock Tower. Six o'clock struck. I was tired of sitting alone, and opening the door of the Secretary's room quietly I entered and took a seat in the shadow.

A Sentence of Death

"It was a strange scene that I had broken in on. Absolute silence prevailed; but both men were so engrossed in thought that my entrance passed quite unnoticed. Matthews was seated in his chair, his elbows on his knees, his head buried in his hands. Stephen, his eyes fixed on the carpet before him, strode to and fro across the room.

"I sat and waited. Outside, the church bells had begun ringing for the evening service, and their music alone broke the heavy silence of the room. Then Matthews spoke briefly, raising a point that had been hammered to weariness before. There was a brief answer from Stephen, and the silence was resumed, Matthews with his head still resting in his hands, Stephen still pacing the floor. Time passed. The bells ceased ringing, seven o'clock struck, and we passed into a soundless quiet. Now and then a question was put and an answer given, but there was no discussion. It seemed that the strange scene might continue until the hangman slipped his bolt next morning. I counted the quarters—one—two—three— eight o'clock. Three hours had gone by and no light had broken on the silent struggle.

"I had ceased to expect any change in this drama of indecision, and resigned myself to an all-night vigil. I sat and speculated as to the course of events. What seemed most probable to me was that the silent drama would go on far into the night and that then in sheer exhaustion there would be surrender. They would not be able to hold out to daylight, and in despair of coming to a decision would choose the way of safety. Presently my ears caught the sound of a

A Sentence of Death

step in the corridor without. It paused at the door. A sudden thought flashed in my mind as I waited for what should follow. There came a low tap at the door, and I hastily opened it. As I did so a messenger handed me a letter. I took it eagerly, raised the flap sufficiently to catch the words, 'I, Lipski, hereby confess . . .' and passed it to Matthews. As he read it he leapt to his feet with a cry as of one who had himself escaped a sentence of death, and for a moment the load lifted from the two men made them almost beside themselves with joy. Then Matthews remembered the circumstances and turned grave. . . .

"The next morning Lipski was hanged, and all the world read the confession. It was Matthews' moment of supreme triumph. He was the minister who had defied the ragings of the Press and the mob and been justified in his firm resistance to ignorant clamour. But none knew the torture behind that firmness, or the misery of those silent hours the night before. How would it have ended without that knock at the door? Ah, who can say? But I think Lipski hanged himself."

ON AN ELDERLY PERSON

AFTER a long walk through Richmond Park and by the Thames one afternoon recently, I went with a companion into a refreshment-place for tea. As we waited for service there entered a tall, stout, elderly gentleman in a tall hat. He took a seat at a table not far off. The face seemed familiar to me, notably the heavy under-jaw that projected with a formidable air of determination. I ransacked my memory a moment, and the identity of the stout, elderly gentleman came back to me vividly. I drew my companion's attention to him, and then raised the second finger of my right hand on which the bone between the first and second joints was palpably enlarged. "That," I said, "is a little memorial which that gentleman in the tall hat gave me forty years ago. He was a good bowler in those days, straight and fast, and a good length, but he had a trick of getting up badly, and when he hit you he hit you hard. One day he hit me in practice when I was playing without a glove, and this is his signature."

But it was not this memory that made the elderly gentleman chiefly interesting to me. It was the fact that he was elderly—so flagrantly elderly. The last time I had seen him he was a stalwart young fellow, quick in his movements, with his head and body

On an Elderly Person

thrust a little forward as though his legs could not quite keep pace with his purpose, and with that formidable chin sticking out as it were in challenge to the future. Now he would have passed for an alderman, "in fair round belly." He moved heavily and slowly like one who had reached whatever goal he had set out after and had no more use for that determined under-jaw. In looking at him I seemed to see myself in a mirror. I must be elderly like that, too. If he were to recognise me as I had recognised him he, no doubt, would be as surprised as I had been to find what an elderly person I had grown into since the days when I was a fresh-coloured youth and we played cricket together.

It is by these reflected lights that the havoc which the years play with us is visible to us. The approach of age is so stealthy that we do not perceive it in ourselves. Others grow old, but we live on under the illusion of unchanging youth. There may be a bald patch on the head; but that is nothing. Quite young fellows have bald patches on the head. That eminent lawyer, Mr. Billson Stork, was bald at twenty-five, and at thirty-five had not a hair above his ears. No, baldness is no evidence. Nor are grey hairs evidence. We all know people who were grey-headed in their early manhood. It is true that we do not run now as we used; but that is simply because we do not want to run. What is there to run for? All these things are discounted by the dissimulating spirit that dwells in us and refuses to let us know that we are visibly taking our place among the old fellows.

On an Elderly Person

Then some incident like that I have described dissipates momentarily the pleasant illusion that defies the calendar. Perhaps someone in the bus, full of good intentions, offers you his seat. You are glad of the seat and you appreciate the kindness, but your feelings are complicated by the suggestion that you bear about you the stigmata of decrepitude. You have become a person whose venerable years entitle you to consideration. You realise, almost with a shock, that to the eyes of that admirable young man in the bus you are an old gentleman whom it would be indecent to leave hanging on to a strap. It is a disillusioning experience, and if the young man could read your mind he would probably conclude that the higher courtesy would have been to keep his seat and leave you your comfortable fancy. There are cases when politeness cuts deeper than impertinence. I myself saw an illustration of this in a bus only yesterday, when a young fellow rose to make room for a very stout lady, although there was a vacant seat beside him. It is true that the stout lady really needed two seats, but she did not want the fact proclaimed in that public way, and her anxiety to point out to the young man that there was still a vacant seat showed that the stout as well as the elderly can nurse illusions about themselves.

But it is in his own family that the sharpest reminders of the cold truth are borne in upon the elderly. There was a time, it does not seem long ago, when you were an Olympian to your children, when the cloud on your brow had the authority of Jove, and the lightest word on your lips was a Delphic

On an Elderly Person

oracle. That phase passed insensibly. You began to measure yourself in your slippers with the new generation. You began to discover that they could wear your boots, and then that they could not wear your boots. A little later and you knew that you had come down from Olympus altogether, and that these young people had ideas which were not your ideas, that they belonged to a new world which was no your old, unchallenged world. They had ceased to be your children and had become something like brothers and sisters. All this accomplished itself so quietly, so naturally, that you did not notice it.

Then, one day, something happens, a trifling action, it may be, a trifling word, an accent, a gesture, but it is enough. It lifts the curtain of your fiction. You know that you have changed places with the children of yester-year. They are no longer your children. They have ceased even to be your brothers and sisters. They are becoming a sort of maiden aunt or benevolent uncle. You realise that to them you have become something of an antiquity, a person who must be humoured because of his enormous past and his exiguous future. You feel that if you are not careful you will be invited to take somebody's arm to steady you. You suspect that your ways are the source of amusement, respectful but undisguised, like the ways of a rather wayward child. In short, you learn that you are no longer the young fellow you have imagined yourself to be, but an elderly person, like any other elderly person of your years. It is not an unpleasant discovery. It may even be a pleasant discovery. And in any case it is only a passing spasm.

On an Elderly Person

The indomitable youth within soon puts the revelation aside. I suspect that he never really does grow elderly, no matter what tales the vesture of decay in which he is clothed may tell about him to the outside world.

TAMING THE BEAR

A WOMAN, sitting behind me on the top of a bus, was explaining to her companion how to manage husbands. She was a strong-minded person and very confident on the subject. She had been married fifteen years, she said, and was satisfied that what she had to learn about taming the bear was not worth learning. As far as I could gather her main thesis was that you must not make too much of the bear. We (I speak as one of the husbands under the scalpel of this formidable woman) must not be encouraged to think that we were little tin gods. We must not be allowed to get the idea that our wives were not independent of us. That was fatal. The more a woman showed that she could paddle her own canoe the more humble and manageable we became.

I gathered, too, that we had to be humoured and even humbugged. We were rather like unruly children who needed to have a lollipop stuffed in our mouth occasionally to keep us quiet and in good humour. It was quite easy to fool us. Only that morning her husband wanted to get up to breakfast. "No," said she, "you stay and have your breakfast comfortably in bed." And he did. "I didn't want him downstairs getting in the way and keeping me talking about this, that and the other. I like to have my breakfast in peace."

As she rattled on I seemed to see the whole tribe

of husbands drooping abjectly before her withering exposure. Things which had been mercifully hidden from me became suddenly clear. That habit of breakfasting in bed, for example. It was an old habit with me, a relic of other days, when I went to bed as the dawn was breaking and the birds were tuning up for a new day. I had continued it with grave twinges of conscience long after the excuse for it had ceased to exist. I had felt it was an inexcusable laziness. I had determined for years to break it. Some day, I had said to myself, I will stop this hedonish self-indulgence. I will set the household an example. I will be up with the lark. I will give the family an agreeable shock. I pictured the delight with which they would hail my astonishing appearance on that never-to-be-forgotten day when I came down to breakfast.

Now the whole deceit was as plain as a pikestaff. Now I understood, thanks to that masterful voice behind me, why my feeble protests, periodically uttered, against having my breakfast in bed had been so kindly repulsed. "Oh no, stay where you are. It's no trouble." And I had stayed, listening to the chirping of the sparrows, reading my book, and taking my tea and toast in comfortable ease. And now I knew the humiliating truth. It was all a blind. I was not wanted—that was the plain English of it. I was given my breakfast in bed in order that I might be kept out of the way. It was not a beautiful act of affectionate thoughtfulness, but an artful policy, a method of getting rid of a domestic nuisance under the disguise of generous indulgence. I own my blood boiled. Never again, I said.

Taming the Bear

Meanwhile, the astounding revelation of the way in which the innocent tribe of husbands was chastened and disciplined proceeded. I learned how we were most effectually fleeced and cozened. You feed the brute first. If you want something particular, a new hat or a sealskin jacket, something that you would not get out of us while we were fierce and hungry, you raise the subject when we are well fed, when the hard lineaments of our august countenance relax and the comforting juices of the body begin to spread a benign influence over our emotions. Then we fall. I learned, too, that in the philosophy of this terrific woman a little judicious jealousy was mixed with the diabolical potion with which we were beguiled. "Nothing wrong, of course, my dear, but it does them no harm to know that we are not enslaved, and that there are other fish in the sea beside themselves."

As I heard the disclosure of the net of intrigue with which we were enveloped I felt that something must be done about it. There must be an exposure. The plot must be shown up. The scales must be lifted from the eyes of the blind and credulous victims who sit passively while their doom is woven about them. But this was only the prelude. There must be a crusade. We must have a Husbands' Defence League, with a slogan, "Down with Delilah," and a banner, illuminated by exclusively masculine hands, bearing the portrait of our patron saint, the estimable John Knox, author of that famous and splendid treatise (which I have not yet read) entitled *First Blast of the Trumpet Against the Monstrous Regiment of Women*. That, said I, was the stuff to give them. Brave old

Taming the Bear

John, the foe of Bloody Mary, hated of Elizabeth, the scourge of the Queen of Scots. Three queens, all of them women and all of them his enemies. Glorious old John!

Meanwhile there must be action at once. My eyes had been opened to the sinister meaning of breakfast in bed. I would deal with that forthwith. I would open my campaign without a moment's delay. To-morrow morning I would certainly get up to breakfast. I would not, of course, give the least hint of the enormous meaning of the act. I would simply get up, just as naturally and unostentatiously as if I were a regular getter-up. I would stroll down negligently, perhaps whistling a bar or two of some familiar air in an absent-minded way that would suggest that I had been doing this sort of thing all my life. If there were comments — as there would be — I would turn them aside with an artful jest. I would not disclose my hand. That would be fatal until I had got my Husbands' Defence League in motion. Then I would open my batteries like thunder. Then the Monstrous Regiment of Women would know the tremendous storm that is foreshadowed when I go down to breakfast to-morrow morning. . . . Grand old John! I shall read your treatise to-night (perhaps). I shall think of you to-morrow when I throw off the coverlet of the sluggard and begin the first skirmish of the campaign. I will not be unworthy of you, old John. There shall be heard in the land again the blast of your trumpet and fear shall invade the heart of Delilah.

OURSELVES AND OTHERS

I WAS playing a game of golf the other day with a man whom I had known in other affairs, but whom I had not met before on the golf links. He is one of those men, of whom I wrote some time ago, who are ridden by one idea to the exclusion of all other ideas. At the moment the thing that filled his mind was the Capital Levy, and it filled it so completely that I fancy he went round the links without ever quite realising what he was about. He would pause in the midst of addressing the ball and resume the argument from some new angle. He would make his tee and forget to put the ball on it while he threw another illuminating ray on the absorbing topic. I tried to divert his attention from the Capital Levy by remarks on the game or the beauty of the day, or anything else that was handy, as a red herring, to draw him off the scent; but it was all in vain. He stuck to his theme as precedents stick to law or barnacles to a ship's bottom.

But it was not the subject that was the chief offence to the day and the occasion. What distressed me most was his unconsciousness of the way he was blocking the course. There were a lot of people on the links, and it was clear to me that we were checking those behind us unduly. I gave him hints—slight at first and broad as day as my temper rose—that we must move more quickly. They fell on ears that did not hear. He patted his tee, and looked up to continue his argument; then his ball would roll off the tee, and he would make another little sand-castle; then a new thought would strike him, and he would stop altogether until he had disclosed it. And all the time I was sensible that curses not loud but deep were being uttered, and quite reasonably uttered, by the people behind us.

Now my friend was not an ill-mannered boor, nor even a selfish person. He was simply unconscious of other people; and although he angered me a great deal at the time, I am not holding him up to reprobation entirely. He seemed to me to have an invaluable quality in an extravagant measure. I was conscious that I envied his stolidity and power of divorcing himself from external influences even while I groaned under his intolerable calm. It was a preposterous situation. He was doing all the mischief and I was suffering all the penalty. It reminded me of the younger Pitt who drank the wine while the Clerk of the House got the headache. I was miserable at holding up the people behind, but my opponent who was holding them up was not even aware that they were there, so absorbed was he in the activities of his own mind.

Within reason, this insensibility to the outside world is a precious gift. Many of the Scotch people have it in an aggravating degree. *J'y suis, j'y reste* is their motto. They have what the Americans love to call "poise," an imperturbable indifference to the emotions of others that is half the secret of their success. They are masters of themselves and are clothed in a good tough skin that makes them proof against all the winds that blow. They are inferior, of course, to the Jews, whose insensibility to the feelings of others sometimes passes belief. It is the heritage no doubt of two thousand years of buffetings by a hostile world, and it enables them to exploit their superior qualities of brain to the maximum. But they are trying and often offensive, even to those of us who loathe the gospel according to Mr. Belloc.

I should be sorry to see this callosity offered as a model; but there is a virtue in it. A too sensitive skin is a heavy handicap in a rough world. There is no more sterilising thing than to be excessively conscious of other people. It is the source of most of our weaknesses and affectations, and of nearly all our insincerities of speech and action. There are some of us who are hardly ever our real selves in our contacts with others. Goldsmith "wrote like an angel but talked like poor Poll," because in the presence of company he lost the rudder of himself and was drowned by the waves of inferior but more aggressive minds. We do and say many foolish and many insincere things because the attractions and repulsions of other personalities play the dickens with our emotions. It was this consideration, I think, that led Hazlitt to rank humility as the lowest of the virtues. He meant that the sense of inferiority subordinated us to the dominion of other minds and defeated the authentic expression of ourselves.

My friend on the golf links, of course, carried

Ourselves and Others

insensibility to others too far. Personality should not be like a reed shaken in the wind. It should be stable and erect, standing four-square to all the winds that blow. But while it should not be worried or deflected by what it thinks others may be doing or saying or feeling, it ought not to be forgetful of the rights and conveniences of others. Nor should it forget those small graces that sweeten our intercourse with others. Take the familiar case of birthdays. It is easy to forget other people's birthdays as we grow older and have many birthdays to remember. It is easy to forget them, because we become indifferent to our own. When the light has gone off the morning hills we have no particular pleasure in reminding ourselves how the shadows are lengthening on our path. Years ago we reached a new milestone with the comfortable feeling that there were any number of milestones ahead, and that to pass another one was rather a gay experience. If anything, we did not pass them speedily enough. We could not make the laggard time keep pace with the hurry of the spirit. But when the milestones stretch far behind us and we can count those in front on the fingers of one or two hands the zest for birthdays is diminished. We may even come to regard them in the light of those "third and final" notices which announce the impatience of the tax-collector at our dilatory ways.

But though we may prefer to forget our own birthdays, we like other people to remember them. We like them to remember the day as an assurance that they remember us. We live by the affections, and our happiness depends much more than we are aware of upon the conviction that we have a place in the hearts and memories of others. If we are unfortunate enough to have outlived that place and to have become negligible laggards on the stage, the fact is mercifully concealed from us on 364 days in the year. But on the 365th day it may be blindingly revealed by a silence that stabs to the heart.

I suppose few of us have escaped the experience in some measure. Perhaps Aunt Anne comes down to breakfast on her birthday morning a little conscious of the day and hoping to receive a more cordial greeting than usual on the occasion from her nephews and nieces, whose birthdays are marked with red letters in her own calendar and celebrated by gifts on which she has spent anxious thought. And the breakfast passes without a word on the subject. If Aunt Anne is a sensible woman she makes allowance for the thoughtlessness of youth and remembers that she was once young and careless herself; but she will be an exceptional woman if she does not feel that something of the brightness has gone out of the day.

These little domestic tragedies mean more to us than we care to admit. The small attentions and civilities we bestow or forget to bestow on each other make the atmosphere in which we move. It is many years since I read *Wuthering Heights*, but I remember how the gloom and oppression which hang about that powerful book are created by such trifling incidents as the meeting of father and son in the morning without a word of greeting. They simply glower at each other and pass to their tasks. It is the graces of conduct that give life its flavour and make it sunny for ourselves, as well as for others. Wordsworth uses the perfect image for them when he says:

> The charities that soothe and heal and bless,
>   Are scattered all about our feet—like flowers.

Even remembering the birthday of a friend may help to keep the garden of the mind in beauty and a reasonable regard for the amenities of the links is no bad discipline of conduct. I would not have my friend hurry his shot from a too acute sense of the people behind. Let him take his time and keep his head. But let him give others their place in the sun.

AN OFFER OF £10,000

I HAD a great and pleasurable shock this morning.
I was deep in drab and perplexed thought about
the muddle the world had got into and, incidentally,
the muddle I was getting into myself, when the postman came and, among other things, brought me a
letter from a gentleman named Rosen. I had never
heard of him before—shouldn't know him if I met
him. Yet he began in this cordial fashion: "Can I
be of any service to you?" My heart leapt up at so
friendly and handsome an inquiry. This was the sort
of man I had dreamt of meeting all my life, a hearty,
kindly fellow, full of melting charity who only asked
to be allowed to help a lame dog over the stile. I
wondered who had told Mr. Rosen about me and
induced him to sit down and write in this warm,
generous spirit. Or perhaps he was a reader who
had been touched by the articles of "Alpha of the
Plough." I imagined him reading one of my most
agreeable little things—one with just a hint of pathos
in it perhaps—and turning to Mrs. Rosen and saying:
"We ought to do something for this charming writer,
my dear. What would you suggest?" And the sensible
woman—just touching her eyes, I think, with the
corner of her handkerchief—replied: "Why not
write to him and ask what he would like?" And Mr.
Rosen exclaimed: "Admirable woman! The very
thing," and hastened to his desk and wrote forthwith.

An Offer of £10,000

But he did not stop at asking whether he could be of any service to me. With a fine sense of delicacy he raised a subject which he knew I might have some hesitation in mentioning myself. "He is sure, being a literary man, to be hard-up," he said to Mrs. R., "and you can tell he is a sensitive fellow who would starve rather than say anything about it. We must make it easy for him to tell us all about it." And Mrs. R., her eyes shining through her tears—for she is a soft-hearted woman—said: "Yes, poor fellow, make it easy for him." So Mr. Rosen, his heart warming towards me, went on: "If an immediate sum of money, £50 to £10,000, would be useful, you can have same at *first interview or per registered post* upon your note of hand—i.e., without security."

When I read this I was amazed. How had he hit the sum so perfectly? Why, it was precisely something between £50 and £10,000 — rather nearer £10,000 than £50—that I *did* want. It seemed like manna dropping from heaven. I called to Jane up the stairs and asked her to come and hear of the splendid luck that had befallen us. I declaimed the letter to her in loud and joyous tones. "However can he have heard of us?" she said. "But I wish he wouldn't say 'same.'" "We must not look a gift-horse in the mouth," I said severely. "These noble-hearted people always say 'same.' 'We send same by even post,' they say, 'but if same is not satisfactory, we will take same back and return money for same.' It is very clear and saves time. We must not be fastidious. We must not let our little literary niceties stand in the way of £10,000. I think I shall take the £10,000.

He doesn't seem to mind whether it's £50 or £10,000, and I mind a great deal."

Jane thought we ought to see the Rosens first, to make sure there was not a mistake. It would be odious if we wrote accepting, took the money, spent it, and then found it was meant for someone else of the same name, who probably needed it more. I said I thought Mr. Rosen would not like this cold and calculating way of meeting his friendly advances. I had now a clear perception of him. He was an elderly, big-hearted man with a flowing white beard. He wanted to do a little good in the world before he left it, and he had chosen me as the humble vessel of his benefaction because he liked my articles in the *Star*. What need was there to go prying into his motives farther? He would certainly not like it. He did not want the thing to be talked about. "Please retain the card (enclosed) as a guarantee of absolute secrecy," he said in his letter. That showed the sort of man he was. He did good by stealth. It was our plain duty to respect his wishes. If he did not want the matter talked about, why should we worry him with inquiries?

I think this consideration had great weight with Jane and removed any lingering scruples she had about taking the money. She accepted my view of Mr. Rosen as a venerable old gentleman of the Cheeryble type who wanted to make people happy, and she agreed that we ought not to put obstacles in his way. In the evening we went for a walk down New Bond Street, where the dear old man lives, and took a survey of the premises of our fairy godfather from the other side of the road. I fancy we caught a glimpse of him at the window, with flowing white beard and skull-cap and velvet jacket and gold-rimmed spectacles, through which his eyes beamed with benevolence upon the passers-by. To-morrow I think I will write and tell him I will accept his kind offer of service. Or perhaps I will call, for the post is very uncertain. But I don't think I will take the £10,000. It would look grasping. I think I will ask him for £5000. And I will promise him, of course, "absolute secrecy."

IN A LUMBER-ROOM

I WENT into the lumber-room glowing with an emotion of apostolic fervour. I would clear out this rubbish of the past. It was a shame that it should cumber the ground when space was so exiguous and rents so expensive. Why, this room, said I to myself (looking sternly meanwhile at the chaos within), would take a bed. At a squeeze it would take two beds. Let in the light and the air, and it would be a bedroom fit for the most delicate sleeper, remote alike from the noise without and the disturbing sounds within. I was not sure I would not claim it for myself. Carlyle would have revelled in a room so impenetrable to the cock's shrill clarion and the clatter of the early morning milk-cans.

By this time my eye had grown accustomed to the dim light within and the rubbish began to take definition. I stooped down. and picked up—a boot. Not an ordinary boot, but a boot of monumental pattern, weighing between two and three pounds, with leather like the hide of a rhinoceros and with huge nails cunningly shaped to grip the rocks. Here and there a nail was missing. I knew where each had gone. The one missing from the right sole was knocked out on the Pillar Rock one winter's day. That one from the heel was left on the Finsteraarjock, and with that reminder all the splendours of the Oberland, the gloom of the Rhone Valley below, the Dom and

In a Lumber-Room

the Matterhorn catching the last rays of the sun beyond, came back with a sudden and vivid glory, like the landscape of a dream. Rubbish! This rubbish? . . . I found the fellow of the boot and put them aside. They must be oiled again and stuffed afresh with oats to keep them in shape. I might yet kick a nail or two out of them before the curtain of the rocks and the glaciers was rung down upon my journeyings.

Undismayed by this check I turned to the lumber again. From the confusion a handle protruded. I seized it and drew out an old and battered cricket-bat. I had not seen it for years, and had long forgotten its existence, but at the touch and sight of it old scenes submerged me like a tide. It was pregnant with secret records that I alone could read. That fracture at the bottom was done—let me see—yes, at far-away Lancaster more than thirty years ago, when I was a casual member of a wandering team playing the asylum staff. And at the hint my mind went a-travelling to the pleasant pastures of the Fylde, with the Lune dreamily flowing by the castled town, and the fine sweep of Morecambe Bay visible to the mind's eye beyond, with the evening light spreading over the tranquil landscape and flushing the distant peaks of Lakeland. . . . And that crack down the middle commemorated Whackerley's terrific feat when, last man in against a village team, he went and smote the bowling like a fury and converted an ignominious defeat . . . But let me tell the story of that heroic day. . . .

Fifteen for nine wickets! The scorer, a heavy youth

In a Lumber-Room

with a straw in his mouth and his shirt-sleeves rolled up to the shoulders, announced the fact to me with undisguised enjoyment. He was sitting on a tussock of grass that served for pavilion, commanding a good view of the wicket that was set in the midst of the undulations of the common. Around him were strewn the hats and coats of the players, a few derelict pads, and two jars of ale.

"Looks like a wash-out," said the scorer as the last man in a purple cap departed from the vicinity of the tussock, smacking his leg with the bat, whether with nervousness or assurance no one could say, for no one had ever seen him bat.

"Well, you never can tell," said the publican. "Cricket's a rum game, and what I says is this: 'You never know when a dark horse'll turn up.'" He had brought up the refreshments at my request, and he was not the man to desert me in a tight place.

It was a tight place. I had challenged the village team, and had got together a scratch lot from anywhere; a boy home from school, elderly persons who "used to play, but haven't touched a bat for years, y'know," a man who had once played for his "house" at Harrow, another whose brother had been twelfth-man for his college, and so on—a team of great expectations, a team that might astonish the countryside or vanish in laughter.

It looked like vanishing in laughter. We had begun very hopefully. The village team had straggled up from the valley straight from the harvest fields that stretched below over the countryside. A few, including Alec, an enterprising young farmer, with

In a Lumber-Room

a round cherubic face, who captained the team, were in flannels; the rest in their harvesting clothes. Alec won the toss and declared that he would take first smack. It was a wicket of fire, outwardly smooth and amiable, but charged with volcanic possibilities that made the ball work miracles, plunging, shooting, bumping, breaking like an untamed colt or an infuriated bull. We missed a catch or two in the first over, but two wickets fell in the second, and when Tom Wilkins, the local Jessop, was run out and six wickets were down for twenty we seemed to have the villagers at our mercy.

We found unsuspected support from an aged umpire —a responsible-looking person with a bowed back and a massive grey beard, sexton, bell-ringer and parson's factotum—who followed one simple rule. Whenever he was appealed to he held up his hand, gravely and benignantly, like a bishop administering a blessing. With his help we got rid of two or three truculent fellows who looked like scoring, and all the team were out for forty-nine. They would have been out for less if I had not, in a weak moment, put Jim Whelks on to bowl. Jim is the local higgler and had assured me that he had captained a team "down in the sheers," and that his bowling—underhand—was such a whirlwind affair that the local men stood in terror of him. "Don't suppose they'll let me bowl, sir," he said, confidentially, the night before. But they did. I wished they hadn't, for his whirlwind piled up twelve byes for them.

It seemed a small thing to score fifty runs. The publican was sure we should do it. "It's a team of

In a Lumber-Room

dark horses," he said to me cheerfully, "and it stands to reason there's one flier amongst 'em." To Alec I fancy he had another tale, for the publican is above party, with a foot planted securely in each camp. But the dark horse did not appear. Our misfortunes began in the first over, and continued with remarkable regularity during the succeeding overs. If anyone looked like making a stand the venerable umpire, pursuing his sovereign rule with inflexible impartiality, held up his hand. Fifteen for nine, and as the last man went in smacking his leg with his bat, we wondered how we were to steal from the stricken field unobserved by the village folk, who were sitting in the shade under the hedge.

But what was this? Purple Cap, who had gone in last because he was so confident that he "wasn't worth a run," had cracked the first ball to the ditch for four and snicked the next for one. Twenty! Well, well, this was not disgraceful. He had the bowling again. The first ball went over the hedge—six; the second bounded down the hill towards the valley—four: thirty. "Well, he is a one-er," said the scorer, changing his straw to the other side of his mouth. Panic seized the bowlers; the fielders went farther and farther out into the landscape. But Purple Cap was insatiable. He seemed not a man but a hurricane. He leapt at everything with a devouring fury and the ball flew here, there, and everywhere. Once the stumper appealed, but he had the wrong umpire for judge. My bat was smashed, but I didn't care. "Send him more bats," I shouted. The score rose like magic. "A regular pelthoria of runs," said the publican.

In a Lumber-Room

Forty—fifty (the match was won)—sixty—seventy—
—eighty—eighty-five—then a well-directed throw-in
from the long-field knocked the wicket down. "How's
that?" Up went the venerable umpire's arm like a
semaphore at the familiar sound. And Purple Cap
came back to the tussock in triumph.

"It was just as I said," remarked the publican
when I saw him standing before the inn later in the
evening. "'Mark my words,' I said, 'there's a dark
horse in that lot somewhere,' and a dark horse there
was. I ain't seen anything like it since my soldiering
days in India. Killed a python we did—dead as a
door-nail down to the last two-foot of his tail. I put
my arm on his tail and he closed round it that tight
you couldn't pull him away until his tail was dead
too. I ain't seen such a lively tail since until I set
eyes on that chap in the purple cap this evening.
He's stirred this place up and no mistake. They won't
forget him in a hurry."

Of course, the bat must remain. It was not a bat,
but a living memorial, a thing that talked to me a
joyous private language and seemed to secrete by
some magic the very essence of myself. To destroy
it would be a sort of suicide. As well might
Nelson have broken up the timbers of the old
Victory to heat the kitchen fire. I rubbed the dust
from its battered face and put it honourably in
the corner.

I began to feel as though I had been caught dese-
crating a cemetery. The vision of that additional
bedroom, with windows, fresh air and electric light,
was fading. I bent a little doubtfully and seized a

In a Lumber-Room

large tome. It was an old album, one of those huge and ugly volumes that no household was without a generation ago, but no household visibly possesses to-day. And I began to turn over its leaves. . . . What is there more poignant than an old, forgotten album? Here are "the children" again, miraculously resurrected from the past, playing on the sands at Dawlish, swimming in the sea, standing against the sky-line of the cliffs at Sheringham with the sunshine upon their laughing faces and their hair streaming in the wind. How long I spent over that old album I do not know, for it stirred many thoughts that made me forgetful—thoughts that do not easily find words to clothe them. But I put the album aside for dusting. Really this lumber-room might be kept more tidily and reverently.

And what is this vast cover, sticking out, dog-eared, from the lumber? My old portfolio, given me forty-six years ago as a tribute from admiring parents to my artistic achievements. How I gloried in its ample blue covers. Why, Landseer himself, the incomparable Landseer, must have such a portfolio as that. And I laboured with my pencil to fill it with things worthy of its dignity, and here they were to-day, old portraits of grandmothers and aunts and copies of Landseer's dogs and horses and Peter Paul in his big hat, and the serene Dürer, with his long flaxen curls, and, on each one, in large, bold, boyish writing, "Drawn by ——" and the date carefully put in lest posterity should not know that these miracles were done by one so young. Ay de mi, as old Carlyle used to say. Ay de mi. . . .

In a Lumber-Room

I have changed my mind about the lumber-room. We have plenty of bedrooms, and if we haven't we must go short. That lumber-room is the abode of finer things than bedsteads. It is a chamber of the spirits. But it must certainly be kept more tidy.

OUR NEIGHBOUR THE MOON

JANE observed just now that she was sure the days were drawing out. We laughed, as we were expected to, at the immemorial remark, but we cheerfully agreed that there was truth in it. We looked at our watches. It was past four and the landscape of half a dozen counties still lay, darkening but visible from the hillside, while in the garden the thrushes were singing as though it were a summer evening. The moon, which had been faintly visible long before the sun had set, was beginning to take up "the wondrous tale." It was that bewitching moment of the day when the two luminaries are about equally matched and the light of the moon filters through the light of the day and a new scheme of shadows begins to take shape about you as you walk.

If I were asked to name the chief difference between living in town (as I used to do) and living in the country (as I now chiefly do), I think I should say that it consisted in the place which the moon fills in our everyday life, especially of course in the dark season of the year. It might almost be said that we do not discover the moon until we live in the country. In town it is only another and a rather larger lamp hung aloft the street. We do not need it to light us on our way and are indifferent to its coming and going. If it shines, well; if it does not shine, no matter. We

Our Neighbour the Moon

go about our business in either case, and do not consult the calendar to know whether such-and-such a night will be light enough to go to the theatre or to dinner with Aunt Anne at Kensington, as the case may be. Nothing but fog can interfere with these amenities and the calendar is uninformed as to the vagaries of the fog.

But in the country the moon is not an unconsidered and casual visitor whose movements are of such little account that we do not trouble to study them. It is, on the contrary, the most important and most discussed neighbour we have. In town we do not think of the moon in neighbourly terms. It is something remote and foreign, that does not come within the scope of our system. We should miss the lamp across the road that sends a friendly ray through our window-curtains all night, and if we went down to Piccadilly Circus one evening and did not see the coloured signs twinkling on the shop-fronts we should feel lonely and bereaved. But if the moon did not turn up one evening according to plan, hardly one Londoner in a thousand would notice the fact. He would read about it in the newspapers next day and talk about it coming up to the City in the tube, but he would not have discovered the fact himself or have been sensible of any loss.

It is otherwise with us country bumpkins. The neighbourliness of the moon and of the stars is one of the alleviations of our solitude. We have no street lamps or pretty coloured sky-signs to look at, and so we look at the Great Bear and Orion, the Sickle and the Pleiades, trace out Cassiopeia's chair and watch

Our Neighbour the Moon

to see Sirius come up over the hilltop like a messenger bearing thrilling tidings. We know they are far off, but there is nothing between us, and intimacy seems to make them curiously near and friendly. A cloudy night that blots out the stars is as gloomy an experience for us as an accident at the electric power-house that puts out the street lights and plunges the house in darkness is to the dweller in Hampstead or Clapham.

But it is the moon that is our most precious neighbour. Its phases are as much a part of the practical mechanism of life as the winding-up of the clock, and the hour of its rising and setting regulates our comings and goings. If it failed to turn up one night all the countryside would know about it. There would be a universal hue-and-cry and no one would sleep in his bed for watching. When the sickle of the new moon appears in the sunset sky the cheerful nights set in. There is no need to light the lantern if we want to go to the wood-shed or to the chicken-run at the end of the garden to investigate some unfamiliar sound that proceeds from thence. If there is anything contemplated at the village schoolroom down in the valley it is fixed for an evening when the moon is high to light us by road or field-path; and when the moon is near the full we reach the high festival of our country nights. Then, no matter how busy the day has been or how comfortable the fireside is, the call of our neighbour the moon to come out and see the magic he can throw over the landscape is irresistible.

It is irresistible now. While I have been writing, the moon has been gathering power. The night is clear and full of stars. There is the glisten of frost on the grass. The wind has fallen and the plain that glimmers below in the moonlight is soundless. It would be a sin not to be abroad on such a night. Moreover Ben and Jeff need a run before settling down for sleep. They love the moonlight too, not for its poetry but for its aid in the ceaseless, but ever unrewarded, task of exploring rabbit-holes and other futile hints of sport. "Come, Ben! Come, Jeff! . . . Walk."

ON SMILES

IF I were to be born into this world again and had the choice of my endowments I should arrange very carefully about my smile. There is nothing so irresistible as the right sort of smile. It is better than the silver spoon in the mouth. It will carry you anywhere and win you anything, including the silver spoon. It disarms your enemies and makes them forget that they have a grudge against you. "I have a great many reasons for disliking you," said a well-known public man to a friend of mine the other day, "but when I am with you I can never remember what they are." It was the flash of sunshine that did for him. He could not preserve his hostility in the presence of the other's disarming smile and gay good-humour. He just yielded up his sword and sunned himself in the pleasant weather that the other carried with him like an atmosphere.

At the Bar, of course, a pleasant address is worth a fortune. I suppose there has been no more successful figure in the law courts in our time than Rufus Isaacs, but I fancy he won as many of his victories by the debonair smile with which he irradiated the courts as by his law. You could see the judge on the bench and the jury in the box basking in the warmth that he shed around them. The weather might be as harsh as it liked outside; but here the sky was

On Smiles

clear and the sun was shining genially. It was a fine day and the only blot on the landscape was the unhappy counsel for the other side, who thumped the table and got red in the face as he saw his client's case melting away like snow before a south wind.

And among politicians it is notorious that a popular smile is the shortest cut to the great heart of democracy. In an estimate of the qualities that have contributed to Mr. Lloyd George's amazing success a high place would have to be given to the twinkling smile, so merry and mischievous, so engagingly frank and so essentially secret and calculating, with which, by the help of the photographer, he has irradiated his generation. If Mr. Asquith had learned how to smile for public consumption, the history of English politics, and even of the world, would have been vastly different; but Mr. Asquith's smile is private and intellectual and has no pictorial value, and I doubt whether anyone ever heard him laugh outright. He was born without the chief equipment of the politician in a democratic age. No one knew the value of that equipment more than Theodore Roosevelt. He was the most idolised public man America has produced for half a century, and he owed his popularity more to his enormous smile than to any other quality. It was like a baron of beef. You could cut and come again. There was no end to it. It seemed to stretch across the Continent from the Atlantic to the Pacific, and when it burst into laughter it shook the land like a merry earthquake. There was not much behind the smile, but it was the genuine article, the expression of a companionable spirit and a healthy

On Smiles

enjoyment of life, and it knocked the Americans "all of a heap." Woodrow Wilson's smile was almost as spacious as Roosevelt's, but it was less infectious, for it was thoughtful and reflective; came from the mind rather than the feelings, and never burst into laughter. It was the smile of the schoolmaster, while Roosevelt's was the smile of the uproarious schoolboy who was having no end of "a bully time."

Really first-rate smiles are rare. For the most part our smiles add little to our self-expression. If we are dull, they are dull. If we are sinister, they are only a little more sinister. If we are smug, they only emphasise our smugness. If, like the Lord High Everything Else, we were born sneering, our smile is apt to be a sneer, too. If we are terrible, like Swift, we shall have his "terrible smile." Only rarely do we light upon the smile that is a revelation. Harry Lauder's smile is like a national institution or a natural element. It is plentiful enough to fill the world. It is a continual and abundant feast that requires neither words nor chorus, and when he laughs you can no more help feeling happy than he can. Lord Balfour's smile is famous in another way. It has the untroubled sweetness of a child's, and there are few who can resist its charm; but it is elusive and seems too much like a mask that has little to do with the real man. You feel that he would send you to the scaffold with the same seraphic sweetness with which he would pass you the sugar. It is not an emanation of the man like that abundant smile, at once good-humoured and sardonic, with which Mr. Birrell sets the company aglow.

On Smiles

The most memorable smiles are those which have the quality of the unexpected. A smile that is habitual rarely pleases, for it suggests policy, and the essence of a smile is its spontaneity and lack of deliberation. Archbishop Temple said he hated people who were always smiling, and then, looking across the luncheon table at the vicar who had been doing his best to ingratiate himself with the terrible prelate, added: "Look at the vicar there—*he's* always smiling." It was a cruel affront, but the smile that has the quality of an artifice is hard to bear. It was so in the case of Mrs. Barbauld, of whom it was said that she wore such an habitual smile that it made your face ache to look at her. One would almost prefer the other melancholy extreme, illustrated by that gloomy fanatic, Philip II., who is said to have laughed only once in his life, and that on receiving the merry news of the massacre of St. Bartholomew. The smiles that dwell in the mind most are those that break suddenly like sunshine from unexpected places. That was the quality of the curiously wistful smile that played over the ascetic features of Lord Morley in conversation. You could forgive all his asperities when he smiled. But the most delightful example of the unexpected smile that I know is that of the pianist, Frederic Lamond. The intensity of his countenance forbids the suggestion of a smile, and at the piano he seems to descend into unfathomable depths of gravity and spiritual remoteness. But when the piece is over and the house breaks out into thunders of applause, he emerges from the depths with a smile that suggests that the Land of Beulah has broken on his sight. It

On Smiles

is so sudden a transition that you almost seem to catch a glimpse of the Land of Beulah yourself.

But it is no use for those of us who have only humdrum smiles to attempt to set up a smile that is an incantation. Smiles, like poets, are born, not made. If they are made, they are not smiles, but grimaces, and convict us on the spot. They are simply an attempt to circulate false news. There is no remedy for us of the negligible smile, but to be born again and to be born different, not outside but within, for the smile is only the publication of the inward spirit.

WHEN IN ROME . . .

I HAVE not seen any reply from a certain distinguished
Englishman who has recently been in America to the
resolution passed by an American women's society,
and published in the Press, denouncing certain alleged
proceedings of his as a moral affront to public opinion
in America. The allegations were to the effect that he
had invited people to drink from his private store of
alcoholic liquor in the ante-rooms of some chapel
where he had been speaking, and that his daughter
had smoked cigarettes in public. Whether the state-
ments were well-founded or an invention of the
Press I do not know, nor for the purpose I have in
view does it matter. The incident interests me, not
as a question of morals but of manners. Morals
are largely a local thing, a question of latitude and
climate, of custom and time. They vary with the
conditions of life and the habit of thought.

When we eat our morning rasher we are conscious
of no moral offence, but to the Jew it would be not
merely a moral offence, but an irreligious act. The
difference is probably traceable to nothing more than
climatic conditions. With us a pig is a perfectly safe
article of diet, but in the East it is a perilous food;
and being also a tempting food it needed the in-
hibitions both of morality and religion to prevent
its consumption. I have no doubt that if the Jewish

When in Rome . . .

religion had originated in the Western world, there would have been no ordinance against pork in it. But while we may regard that ordinance as irrelevant in this country, we should be wanting in good manners if, on inviting a Jew to dinner, we offered him nothing but a varied choice of pig's meat. We may consider his morality absurd, but we have no right to flout it because we do not approve of it.

And the same thing, I think, applies to those who visit foreign countries. It is their business to respect the morals and conventions of those countries even if they do not share them or like them. It is, for example, one thing for an American citizen who loves wine and liberty to denounce Prohibition in his own country, and quite another thing for a stranger on a visit to show disrespect to the law of the land, however mistaken he may regard it. It seems silly to us to try to get morally indignant at women smoking cigarettes. It has become a commonplace which we accept without comment. But it is not long since such a thing would have been undreamed of in our world, and when a visitor from abroad who did it deliberately would have given great and very proper offence. The axiom "When in Rome do as Rome does" is a counsel of civility. It does not mean that it is our duty to kiss the Pope's toe or adopt the moral code of Rome ourselves; but it does mean that we should not scoff at Roman ways or publicly, or semi-publicly, indicate that we dislike them.

When I go to a foreign country I do my best to be inconspicuous, and to pass myself off as one of the people. I do not succeed, for I happen to be an

When in Rome . . .

insular person, who carries the marks of his origin on him in every gesture, accent and movement. If I dislike a law in my own country and think it should be altered, I have no hesitation in holding it up to opprobrium, and even breaking it, if only in that way can it be successfully fought. But it would be an impertinence on my part to go to France and defy the liquor laws of that country because I did not think they were stringent enough, or denounce the inspection of women because I think it is a loathsome practice, liable to the vilest insults and misuse. French morality accepts these things, and I have no right of interference if I go there.

I am not sure that I even like moral missionaries from one country to another. The offence, if it is an offence, is in a different category from that of the man who publicly flouts the laws and customs of another land in which he happens to be a visitor; but it certainly borders on bad manners. I express no opinion about "Pussyfoot" Johnson's gospel, but I confess I always feel an irritation at his intrusions here. However much I wanted the country to be converted to his point of view, I should still wish that he would stay at home and cultivate his own garden, and leave us to look after our own morals and practices. And by the same token I should resent the idea of a person going from this country to America and openly flouting its public morality, or taking sides in a domestic controversy that happened to be raging there. In short, it is a question not of morals, but of manners.

I do not think the idea I have in my mind could be better illustrated than by a famous story of

When in Rome . . .

Spurgeon. I daresay it is familiar to some of my readers, but it is so apposite and so good that they will not object to renew its acquaintance. In the days of his unparalleled popularity, when the great preacher filled the Tabernacle from floor to ceiling, it was the custom of the young bucks sometimes to show by their ill-manners their contempt for something they did not understand. One night three of them went into the gallery with their hats on, and refused to remove them when the attendant requested them to do so. Spurgeon watched the incident, and when the preliminaries of the service had been concluded and the time came for the sermon, he prefaced his remarks with something like these words: "In all the occasions of life it is our duty and should be our pleasure to respect the feelings of others and the customs of others, even if we do not share them. The other day I went into a Jewish synagogue and, according to my practice when entering a place of worship, I removed my hat. But, having done so, an attendant came to me and reminded me that in the Jewish synagogue it was necessary that the head should be covered. I thanked him and, of course, obeyed the reminder. Now" (looking up to the gallery and raising his voice) "will those three young Jews in the gallery show that respect to the customs of this place of worship which I showed to theirs?"

THE JESTS OF CHANCE

THERE is one story in Field-Marshal Sir William Robertson's autobiography that is sure of a place among the legends of celebrated men. It is that in which he tells by what a lucky accident he was saved, when "a raw recruit," from deserting from the Army, of which he was destined to become one of the most illustrious ornaments. Another young private who occupied a bed in the room in which he slept stole the civilian clothes in which Robertson contemplated making his escape, and vanished. I daresay Robertson said some harsh things at the time about the thief, who had put temptation out of his way; but he must have thanked him almost every day of his life since. For in taking away Robertson's clothes the thief had put a field-marshal's baton in his knapsack.

Not many of us have the luck to become field-marshals through the purloining of our trousers, but few of us are without experience of the part which trifles that seem of small moment at the time play in our careers. "Character," says Victor Hugo, "is destiny," and a greater than Hugo has observed that it is not in our stars but in ourselves that we are thus and thus. This is no doubt true, though the doctrine may be carried too far. For example, I think that Hazlitt is a little unjust to Charles James Fox when

The Jests of Chance

he says that the history of his failure is written in his fluctuating chin. I doubt whether, if the parts had been reversed, Pitt would have done any better. But no one can compare the easy, good-natured profile of Fox with the haughty masterfulness of Pitt's without knowing which of the two would win in an encounter of will-power where the circumstances were even.

I remember Lord Fisher once describing to me with great admiration a wonderful feat of navigation by which that famous sailor, Admiral Wilson, had brought the fleet through great perils in a fog, fighting all the way with his obstinate chief officer over charts and calculations. "But Wilson had his way," said Fisher. "You see, his jaw stuck out half an inch farther than the other fellow's." There is much virtue in a jaw that will stand no nonsense. You can read the whole history of the most wonderful one-man achievement in the annals of trade in the stubborn chin of Lord Leverhulme, just as you can read the tale of Mr. Balfour's political purposelessness in his amiable but indecisive countenance. "I can see him now," wrote a friend quoted in Mrs. Drew's *Some Hawarden Letters*. "I can see him now, standing at the top of the great double staircase, torn with doubts which way to go down. 'The worst of this staircase,' he would say, ' is that there is absolutely no reason why one should go down one side rather than the other. What am I to do?'"

But though destiny is much a matter of chins, the Imp of Chance who comes in and steals our trousers has no small part in determining our lives and shaping

The Jests of Chance

events. I have read that Wallenstein in his youth had a crack on the head which he, no doubt, felt was a misfortune, but it gave him just the surgical treatment that converted him from a dullard into a great general. Loyola got wounded in battle, and, thanks to that circumstance, found his true vocation and became the creator of the greatest religious order in history, and, with Luther, perhaps the greatest maker of history for six centuries. Newton, according to the legend, sees an apple fall and starts a train of thought that reveals one of the profoundest secrets of the universe. I suppose no one who has advanced far in life can fail to recall trifles that shaped the whole course of his career—a broken engagement, a misdirected letter, a chance meeting. At the time it seemed nothing, and now, in the retrospect, it is seen to have meant everything. The chin may dictate events within limits, but the Imp of Chance has as often as not the final word.

There is an interesting speculation on the theme of what might have happened in Mr. Asquith's book on the origin of the war. Referring to the appointment of Baron Marschall von Bieberstein as German Ambassador to London in 1912 and his death a few months later, he says that he is confident, so far as one can be confident in a matter of conjecture, that if Marschall had lived there would have been no European War in 1914. I fancy that is a common view in informed quarters. Marschall stood intellectually, as well as physically, head and shoulders above the petty men with whom the Kaiser had surrounded himself, and it is inconceivable that he would have allowed his country to drift into war under an entire misapprehension as to the mind and power of this country.

It is in this way that the chapter of accidents plays havoc with the affairs of men. All the woes of Ilium sprang from an elopement, and it is a commonplace that if Cleopatra's nose had been a shade longer—or shorter, for that matter—the whole story of the ancient world would have been altered. I suppose the most momentous political event in the history of the last thousand years was the rupture between England and America, which is said to have happened as the result of a shower of rain. But for that rupture, the British Commonwealth to-day would include the whole North American Continent, and its word would be sovereign over the earth. Perhaps the seat of authority would have been in Washington, instead of London, but wherever it was it would have stabilised this reeling world and given its people a security that now seems unattainable. The speculation which attributes the enormous calamity of the loss of America to a shower of rain is more fanciful, but hardly less reasonable, than that which Mr. Asquith advances in regard to the European War. The Earl of Bute was the evil genius of George III., and the inspiration of his disastrous policy. And the origin of his sinister power was a storm at Epsom which kept the royal party from going home. The Prince of Wales needed someone to make up a hand at cards to pass the time while the shower lasted, and Bute, then a young man, being handy, was selected, and from that incident ingratiated himself with the Prince and still more with the Prince's wife. She established his influence over her son whom later, as George III., he led into the ruinous part of personal government which culminated in the Boston Tea Party, the War of Independence, and the Republic of the Stars and Stripes.

Chance does not, of course, always play a malevolent part like this. It sometimes works as if with a superb and beneficent design. Lincoln, on the threshold of fifty, regarded himself as having failed in life and he died at fifty-six, one of the world's immortals. It was the quite unimportant incident of his debate with Douglas that threw him into prominence on the eve of the crisis which, but for his wisdom and magnanimity, would have left America like Europe, a group of warring States. But in the end chance betrayed him. On the night he was murdered the faithful guardian who had shadowed and protected him throughout the war was sick, and his place was taken by a substitute who became absorbed in the play, and allowed Booth to slip unseen into the President's box and fire the fatal shot. But it might be argued that even in this felon betrayal, chance only completed the splendour of its design, for Lincoln's work was done, and it was the circumstances of his death that threw the nobility of the man into relief for all time.

And while the accidents of life so often seem to take control of events, it is no less true that our most deeply calculated schemes sometimes turn round and smite us. When Queen Victoria's eldest daughter married the King of Prussia's eldest son, it was

The Jests of Chance

universally agreed that a grand thing had been done for the peace of the world, and when later a child was born, the rejoicings in London, as you may read in the contemporary records, were like those that welcome a great victory. That child was the ex-Kaiser William, now an exile in Holland. In the light of to-day those rejoicings of sixty odd years ago read like a grim comment on this queer and inexplicable world.

It is one of the agreeable features of the diverting adventure of life that our triumphs so often come clothed in misfortune and that the really big things that happen to us take the shape of trifles. Whenever we are tempted to inveigh against things that go wrong, we might do worse than remember the Field-Marshal's trousers.

IN DEFENCE OF "SKIPPING"

A FEW days ago Mr. Chesterton expressed a doubt whether he had ever read Boswell "through." Knowing Mr. Chesterton, and having a life-long acquaintance with Boswell, I share his doubt. G. K. C. has an amazing gift for seizing the spirit and purport of a book by turning over the pages in handfuls and sampling a sentence here and there. He treats books as the expert wine-taster treats wines, not drinking them in great coarse gulps, but moistening his lips and catching the bouquet on his palate. The parallel is no doubt as misleading as most parallels are apt to be. Good wines have to be "tasted" in this way, but the better the book the deeper should be the draught or the more deliberate and patient the mastication. "Chewed and digested" is Bacon's phrase.

But I am far too much addicted to "skipping" myself to treat the practice as a crime in others. When I was young and industrious and enthusiastic I read as solemnly and slavishly as anyone. I was like a dog with a bone. The tougher the theme the more I exercised my intellectual molars on it. Stout fellows like Zimmermann *On Solitude*, and Burke on *The Sublime and Beautiful*, and Mill *On Liberty* were the sort of men for my youthful ardour. I cannot honestly say I enjoyed them, but I can honestly say that I read them, and I can also honestly say that I shall

In Defence of " Skipping "

never read them or their like again. I finished my drudgery long ago, and have become a mere idler among books, a person who has served his apprenticeship and can go about enjoying himself, taking a sip here and a longish "pull" there, passing over this vintage, and returning to that and generally behaving like a freeman wandering over the estates of the mind, without a duty to anything but his own fancy.

I, too, doubt whether I have read Boswell through. Why should I read it through? I have read the conversations a hundred times and I hope to read them a hundred times more; but I will make no affidavit about the letters. I suspect that I have been "skipping" the letters unconsciously all my life. And *Paradise Regained*? My conscience is clear about *Paradise Lost*, and I can still mouth the speeches of the first author of our misfortunes whom the judgment of time had converted into the hero of that immortal poem. But can I put my hand on my heart and say I have read the *Regained* right through? I cannot. I am not even sure that I have read Shakespeare through. I have a vague notion that in the lusty youth of which I have spoken I did read *Titus Andronicus* and *Pericles* with the rest, but I am quite prepared to believe that I only like to believe I did.

There is high precedent for those of us who "skip." Johnson himself was a famous "skipper," and confessed that he seldom finished a book. It is true that he performed the amazing feat of rising two hours before his usual time to read Burton's *Anatomy of*

In Defence of " Skipping "

Melancholy. He was a truthful man, or I should find difficulty in believing him. Of course the achievement was not so great as it seems, for though Johnson believed in early rising on principle and recommended all young men to practise it, he did not himself rise until noon. But the idea of getting up, if only at ten in the morning, with a feverish desire to read Burton tries my faith even in Johnson's veracity. It is pleasant to dip occasionally into that astonishing rag-box of learning, but most of us are as likely to read Bradshaw's Time Table through as Burton's *Anatomy* through. It is not a book; it is a curiosity.

It is a common experience to find that the habit of "skipping" grows on us as we grow older. It is not merely that we are more tired or more lazy: it is that we are more discreet and more delicate in our intellectual feeding. It is with reading as with eating. When we are young we can eat anything. If we are offered a bun before dinner we express no astonishment, but consume it recklessly. But, grown older and wiser, as Holmes remarks, we receive the offer of a bun before dinner with polite surprise. And so with books. When the magic of Shelley seizes us at seventeen we can devour *The Revolt of Islam* as we devoured that large boggy bun, but later we learn to discriminate even with Shelley, and to take great spaces of him as read. And even the most fervent Wordsworthian would admit that his reading of Wordsworth is patchy, and that if the poet had not written a line after he left Grasmere for Rydal Water, his indebtedness to him would not have been sensibly diminished. Who, for example, can honestly say that

In Defence of " Skipping "

he has traversed the Sahara of the *Ecclesiastical Sonnets*?

This is not a plea for skimpy reading. It is good for the young to worry their bone even if there is little meat on it. I would have them serve an arduous apprenticeship in the great world of books, cleaving their own way laboriously through the wilderness. The anthology business for the young is a little over-done. The youthful digestion ought not to be weakened by an exclusive diet of "elegant extracts," and spoon-feeding robs us of the joys of discovery and adventure. What delight is there like encountering in the wilderness some great unknown of whom we have never heard? It is like coming into a fortune, or rather it is better than coming into a fortune, for these are "riches fineless" that grow with compound interest and are not subject to the vicissitudes of things. I found a young maiden of my acquaintance the other day in a mood of unusual exaltation. She had fallen in love and was hot with the first rapture of passion. She had encountered *Emma* and was aflame with ardour for more adventures in the serene world that Jane Austen had opened out before her. That is the way, casual and unsought, that the realms of gold should be invaded. Youth should be encouraged to fashion its own taste and discriminate for itself between the good, the better and the best. When that is done we can "skip" as we like, with an easy mind and a good conscience. We have learned our path through the wilderness. We know where the hyacinths grow and where we can catch the smell of the wild thyme, and the copse where the nightingale sings to the moon. And if with this liberty of knowledge we "skip" some of the high-brows, and are found more often in the company of Borrow than of Bacon—well, we have done our task-work and are out to enjoy the sun and the wind on the heath.

AN OLD ENGLISH TOWN

It was a wish of Seneca's that the wise and virtuous when they slept could lend their thoughts and their feelings out to less wise and less virtuous people. It would be equally admirable if we could occasionally let our spiritual selves take wing and go on holiday, leaving the body at home to carry on the routine business, receive callers, answer the telephone, pay the bills, and so on. If it were possible for me to take such a holiday I should go to Tewkesbury, where the eighth centenary of the famous Norman church of that town is being celebrated. There was a time when I had no desire to go to Tewkesbury. It was one of the places I did not want to go to because I feared that seeing it would destroy the Tewkesbury of my fancy. No one would hesitate to go to a place like Birmingham or Glasgow, for their names awaken no emotions in the mind, and experience of them can shatter no pleasant images.

But Tewkesbury is a name to conjure with. It belongs to the poetry of things. It is entangled in history and comes with the pomp of trumpets and the echoes of far-off deeds. It has the tang of Shakespeare about it. Was it not with its name that that great star swam into our ken with the earliest of our remembered lines?—

> . . . false, fleeting, perjured Clarence
> That stabbed me on the field by Tewkesbury.

An Old English Town

Observe, not "the field at Tewkesbury" or "of Tewkesbury," but "the field by Tewkesbury." A subtle difference, but enough to convince anyone who has been to that field that Shakespeare wandered there in his young days, perhaps boating thither from Stratford some summer day with Ann Hathaway. Was it not Tewkesbury's mustard that Falstaff hurled at Poins—or was it Pistol? "His wits are as thick as Tewkesbury mustard," he said. I like to think that Falstaff stayed at the "Hop Pole" at Tewkesbury on that famous recruiting journey into Gloucestershire, when he ate a pippin in Squire Shallow's orchard, and that it was the mustard he got there that made his eyes water and stuck in his memory. It was certainly at the "Hop Pole" that Mr. Pickwick stopped for dinner on his journey from Bath. That is the last time, I think, that anything important happened at Tewkesbury. Since then it has slept, and one liked to think it was sleeping in a beautiful mediæval dream, undisturbed by anything more modern than an occasional stage-coach or the horn of the red-coated huntsman clattering through the street.

That was how I liked to think of Tewkesbury, and I stayed away from it, lest I should find it was all cinemas, fried-fish shops and tin tabernacles. But one day last summer I was journeying by road from Wales and found Tewkesbury in my path, and that it was convenient to stay like Mr. Pickwick at the "Hop Pole." And now I know that Tewkesbury is as good as its name, and that I can go there and see as perfect a bit of old England as can be seen from the

An Old English Town

Tamar to the Tweed. Of course, a city like York will give you infinitely more, layer on layer of history written on its stones, telling of the England of the Britons, of the Romans, the Saxons, the Normans, and so onward.

But these are remains—the splendid litter of the centuries. The wonderful thing about Tewkesbury is that it is a living whole, a single town of Tudor England left apparently almost untouched—certainly unspoiled. Fifteenth- and sixteenth-century timbered houses, with their upper floors overhanging the pavements, line the three broad compact streets, and between these reverend buildings little doorways admit to multitudinous courts where the poor live. I daresay it oughtn't to be so. I daresay the courts ought to be swept away and the people housed with gardens far afield. But at this moment I am not a social enthusiast, but a lover of the picturesque, and no doubt it is this compact structure of the place that has kept it so perfect a survival of the past. By the gardens and the courts flows Shakespeare's Avon, and just beyond the town it joins the broad flood of the Severn near the Bloody Field where the Wars of the Roses ended—a place of rank grass, left, I was told, untouched since that day of slaughter, nearly half a thousand years ago. "They're afeard o' what they might find," said the old man who directed me. And over all is the great Abbey Church, next to Durham Cathedral perhaps the finest piece of Norman ecclesiastical architecture in England. Thither from the Bloody Field on that day of battle long ago were borne the corpses of the two rivals, and there their bones lie side by side, preaching, for those who care to hear, more potent sermons on the fitful fever of life than ever came from the pulpit.

And this beautiful town is set in a landscape as gracious as "a melody that's sweetly played in tune" —a wide, rich vale, the most fertile part of England. The sun comes up over the Cotswolds in the morning, and sets over the great range of the Malverns in the evening. Between these two sheltering ramparts Tewkesbury lies, dreaming of the Middle Ages. I daresay it has its worries like any other place. But I refuse to be a realist about Tewkesbury. I will indulge my love of romance. I will remember only that as I came away from the "Hop Pole" a vehicle with four jolly-looking fellows inside came up tooting a horn that played old-fashioned airs, and bringing in its train a swarm of boys. And as the boys gathered round the car one of the jolly-looking fellows put his hand in his pocket and drew out a heap of coins that he scattered among them. It was in the true spirit of the place. I fancy Mr. Pickwick did the same thing when he left the "Hop Pole," and I am sure that Falstaff did—in spite of the mustard. I would have done the same thing myself, if I had had the courage and the coppers. The next time I go to Tewkesbury I will fill my pockets with coppers.

ON PEOPLE WITH ONE IDEA

I was travelling down to Devonshire the other day when I met a man in the train with whom I fell into conversation. It was a wonderful day. We had left the fog behind us in London and the country-side glowed, rich and warm, under the sunshine of a cloudless November day. It seemed an occasion on which one could have found a thousand agreeable things to talk about, but I noticed that wherever the conversation with the stranger started it always got round to the taxation of land values. Now I happen to be in favour of the taxation of land values. It is a question about which my mind is as clear as it is about anything in this perplexing world. I am prepared to vote in favour of it in due season and to speak in favour of it when I think any useful purpose can be served. But I confess I got painfully bored by this well-meaning man and that I hailed the opportunity of going to the restaurant car to lunch with secret thanksgiving. I don't think I shall ever be caught *tête-à-tête* with that missionary of the One Idea again. I have got him on the list of People I Can Do Without.

It is a list made up largely of those who wear a bee in their bonnet. There is no surer prescription for the Complete Bore than the tyranny of an idea. We flee instinctively from the man who is always telling us the same thing, who comes into the circle with one ceaseless theme, to which he hitches the

On People with One Idea

heavens above and the earth beneath, and the waters under the earth. There is that excellent publicist, Vernon Pizzey, for example. You have but to say "Good day" to him in the street, and he will buttonhole you, and, with the abstracted air of one who has seen a vision, will open the flood-gates of Birth Control upon you.

When I first knew him he was the passionate pilgrim of Prohibition. Banish alcohol from the face of the earth, and all the problems of life would be solved, and sorrow and sighing would flee away. He has passed out of that phase. It is no longer the abolition of Drink that lights the fires of fanatical faith in his eyes: it is the Abolition of Children. The New Jerusalem which he will build in England's green and pleasant land will have no children playing in its streets. When he hears of a childless home, a ghost of a smile flits over his features, and when he hears of a family of six he looks as though he has heard of some unmentionable sin. He dreams of a golden age when the propagation of children among the poor will be a punishable offence, and when the people of whom he does not approve will be sterilised by order of the court. His prophet is Dean Inge.

I am not concerned here with the merits of his obsession. I refer to him only as an example of those who are ridden by an idea. An idea may be good or bad, but no idea is good enough to claim one's whole waking thoughts. We like people who have many facets to their minds, who hold strong opinions on a variety of subjects and know how to keep them under control, airing them when they are in season

On People with One Idea

and putting them in cold storage when they are not
of season. We like them to think in many quantities,
to let their thought range over the whole landscape
of things, to have plenty of windows to their mind
and to open them in turn to all the winds that blow.
We ought not to be the slave of one idea, but the
master of legions which we should exercise and discipline and from which we should extract a working
philosophy of life. However good the text we ought
not always to be preaching a sermon from it. I
remember when I was a boy a most excellent man, a
lawyer, who, every evening in the week, would take
his stand on the plinth of a Sebastopol cannon in
front of the Shire Hall that faced down the High
Street of the country town in which I lived, and from
thence would exhort the passers-by to repentance.
No one ever heeded him, no one ever even paused to
listen to him, and he lives in my memory a solitary
figure weighed down with the wickedness of men,
giving his life unselfishly to the delivery of his un-
regarded message, a man whose very agony had
become a town jest.

Life is a multitudinous affair, and we suspect the
sanity of a mind which is chained to one idea about
it. I remember leaving the House of Commons on
that tremendous day, the 3rd of August, 1914, when
Sir Edward Grey had just made a speech that
announced the most world-shaking event in history.
In a few hours we should be involved in the greatest
war the world had ever seen. An acquaintance of
mine left the House with me, and as we seated ourselves in a cab he turned to me and said, "Did you

On People with One Idea

see that outrageous vivisection case down at Wigan?"
—or some such place. I forget what I answered, but
I remember the strange feeling that came over me
that I was cooped up with Mr. Dick. Here was the
old, kindly world we had known for a lifetime plunging
down into the gulf of unimaginable things. And beside
me, indifferent to all the enormous happening, was
Mr. Dick, his mind tortured with the wicked doings
down at Wigan, or wherever it was.

There is of course another side to the shield of
the man with One Idea. He could make out a good
case for himself and I think I could make out a good
case for him. The mere fact that his passion is disinterested is alone enough to command respect in
a world where disinterested enthusiasm is a rare
commodity. He is of the stuff of martyrs. He is prepared to die for his idea, or what is harder, to take
the whips and scorns of men who are often, spiritually,
not fit to black his boots. It is his uncalculating passion
that keeps the flame of ideas burning in a dark world.
Without him our moral currency would be sadly
depreciated and the quality of the general life would
lose its salt and savour. I often admire his singleness
of purpose. I sometimes even envy a disinterested-
ness which leaves me ashamed by comparison. But
I do not want to spend a week-end with him and I
will not travel down to Devonshire with him if I
can find a seat in the luggage-van or standing room
in the corridor.

TO AN UNKNOWN ARTIST

IT is certainly an unequal world. As I was crossing
Piccadilly Circus yesterday my eye fell on a man at
work on the building that is being pulled down at
the corner of Regent Street, next to the "Criterion." [1]
He was standing on a fragment of wall of the disem-
bowelled building that still jutted out a few yards
from the side of the "Criterion," which rose like a
vertical precipice beside him, without foothold or
handhold that a squirrel could cling to. He was
perhaps fifty feet from the ground. The width of the
wall was, I suppose, a foot—just space enough for
heel and toe to find standing-room. He was armed
with a pick-axe, and with it he was cutting away the
fragile buttress from underneath his feet. His body
rose and fell with the strokes of the pick-axe. When he
had loosened some portion of the wall, he would
stand on one foot and scrape away the debris with
the other. As it fell rattling to the ground a cloud of
dust boiled up, smothering him and partially hiding
him from view. Then he would turn to with the
pick again, loosen another portion, and repeat
the operation.

I stood and watched him with respect bordering
on admiration. I could not help reflecting what a
helpless figure I should have cut in his place and what

---

[1] The vacant site is now covered by a new block of buildings.

To an Unknown Artist

a short time I should be there. I have been proud of my modest achievements on the rocks, but here was a man who made those achievements seem silly, and he did it as unconcernedly as if he were hoeing potatoes in his garden. Presently he straightened his back, loosened his shoulders, paused, threw a glance up at the vertical cliff above him, and another down the vertical cliff below him, and then resumed.

So I saw him cut away row after row of the brick-work on which he stood. There was a drop of fifty feet, "straight as a beggar can spit," back and front of him—not an inch of room for the play of his feet. Every movement had to be true to the fraction of an inch. Every piece of brickwork he removed involved a new problem within the same inexorable limits. The slightest mistake, and he would plunge down to the rubbish below, and a coroner's jury would say "Accidental death," and that would be the end of his story. Perhaps there would be two lines about him at the bottom of a newspaper column, but nobody would read it, for everybody would be so busy reading how Mr. Kid Lewis put Mr. Frankie Burns to sleep, and how Abe Mitchell did the fourth hole in two, and why Hobbs or somebody else was not caught in the second over.

And this man, rising and falling with the blows of his pick-axe up there on the fragment of wall, is not doing this perilous job occasionally. He is doing it every day. All his working life is spent on some such giddy task as this, swaying to and fro with his axe between a drop of fifty feet on one side and fifty feet on the other. He must never forget—for a moment.

To an Unknown Artist

He must never be dizzy—for a moment. He must be prepared for any sudden gust of wind that blows. As I watched him he seemed to assume the proportions of a great artist. He seemed to become heroic —a figure carrying his life lightly on that frail ledge of the vertical cliff. I daresay it had never occurred to him to think of himself in either rôle. Yet the mere skill of the man was more delicate than the skill of the rather dull cricketers I saw at Lord's on Saturday. There were 12,000 people standing round hour by hour to watch Lee and Haig pile up the stupendous total of fifty runs inside two hours. I do not blame the spectators. I was one of them myself, and very dull I found it. But nobody bothered to give a glance at the figure swaying to and fro on the crumbling wall. Yet as a mere exhibition of skill it was not inferior to the pedestrian play at Lord's or to a skipping match between Carpentier and Dempsey at £1000 a minute. And remember, he was not engaged in a sham fight. He had a drop of fifty feet back and front. Instant death on either side all the time.

But then he was only doing useful work. I wondered what he got for risking his life every hour of every day. Perhaps as much in a week or a month as the *Star* will pay me for writing this article about him. Perhaps as much in a year as an eminent counsel will pocket for a day's "refresher." Perhaps as much in a lifetime as Monsieur Carpentier will take for ten minutes' running exercise with Dempsey in the ring, winding up with a tap in the stomach, a count-out, a handshake (and a wink). No; on second thoughts, not half that, not quarter that.

To an Unknown Artist

When I passed through Piccadilly Circus in the evening the man had gone. So had the fragment of wall on which he stood. You may see the mark of the place where the wall rose on the side of the "Criterion." It is the mark of an unknown artist to whom I offer this tribute of my admiration.

ON LIVING FOR EVER

FOR some time past I have noticed on the hoardings of London a placard illustrated with the picture of an American gentleman named Rutherford, who is represented lifting a prophetic fist in the manner of the advertisements of Horatio Bottomley before that prophet of the war had the misfortune to be found out, and declaring that there are "thousands in this city who will never die." I have not had the curiosity to attend his meetings or to inquire into the character of his revelation. I do not know, therefore, whether I am likely to be one of the people whom Mr. Rutherford has his eye upon. But the threat which he holds over my head has led me to look the possibility in the face. I suppose Mr. Rutherford is satisfied that it is an agreeable possibility. He would not have come all the way from America to tell us about it if he had not thought it was good news that he was bringing.

I think he is mistaken. Judging from my own reactions, as the Americans would say, to his prophecy, I fancy the general feeling would not be one of joy but of terror. If anything could reconcile us to the thought of death it would be the assurance that we should never die. For the pleasure as well as the pathos of life springs from the knowledge of its transitoriness.

On Living for Ever

All beauteous things for which we live
By laws of time and space decay.
But oh, the very reason why
I clasp them is because they die.

All our goings and comings are enriched with the
sense of mortality. All our experiences are coloured
by the thought that they may return no more. Rob
us of the significance of the last words of Hamlet
and the realm of poetry would become a desert,
treeless and songless. It is because "the rest is
silence" that the smallest details of our passage
through life have in them the power of kindling
thoughts such as these:

Sweet Chance, that led my steps abroad,
    Beyond the town, where wild flowers grow—
A rainbow and a cuckoo, Lord,
    How rich and great the times are now!
        Know, all ye sheep
        And cows, that keep
On staring that I stand so long
    In grass that's wet from heavy rain—
A rainbow and a cuckoo's song
    May never come together again;
        May never come
        This side the tomb.

It is not alone the beauty of the sunset that touches
us with such poignant emotion: it is because in the
passing of the day we see the image of another passing
to which we move as unfalteringly as the sun moves
into the shadow of the night. When in these autumn
days we walk in the woodlands amid the patter of
the falling leaves, it is the same subtle suggestion that
attunes the note of beauty to a minor key. Through
the stillness of the forest there echo the strokes of

On Living for Ever

a distant axe felling some kingly beech. For seventy, perhaps a hundred years it has weathered the storms of life, and now its hour has come and in its falling there is the allegory of ourselves. I think it is that allegory that makes my neighbour so passionately conservative about his trees. They stand too thick about his grounds, but he will not have the axe laid to one of them.

We cannot go an unusual journey without a dim sense of another journey from which we shall not return, nor say a prolonged "good-bye" without the faint echo in our minds of ultimate farewells. And who ever left the old house that has sheltered him so long and grown so familiar to sight and touch without feeling some shadow pass across the spirit that is more than the shadow cast by bricks and mortar? Life is crowded with these premonitions and forebodings that make our pleasures richer by reminding us that they are terminable.

And such is the perversity of human nature that if Mr. Rutherford should turn out to be well-informed, those of us who are marked down for deathlessness would find that the pleasure of life had vanished with its pathos. We should be panic-stricken at the idea of never coming to an end, of never being able to escape from what Chesterfield called "this silly world," and Salisbury "this miserable life." We should yearn for death as the condemned prisoner yearns for life or the icebound whaler for the spring. We do not want to die now, but to be comfortable we want to know that we shall die some day. Being under sentence of death we cling to life like limpets to a rock, but if we were sentenced to life we should shrick for the promise of death. We should hate the sunset that we were doomed to see for ever and ever, and loathe the autumn that mocked us with its falling leaves.

I remember that in one of her letters Lady Mary Wortley Montagu remarks that she is so happy that she regrets that she cannot live three hundred years. We all have moments like that, moments when life seems so good that we envy the patriarchs and would be glad if we could abide here longer than Nature permits. But in our gayest moments we could not contemplate the prospect of seeing in the New Year of, let us say, 10024 A.D., with the certainty that we were destined to wait on for the New Year of 100024 A.D., and so on to the crack of doom. The mind would reel before such an enormous vista. We should stagger and faint at the prospect of a journey that had no end and of a future as limitless and unthinkable as space. We should look into the darkness and be afraid. There may be an infinite destiny for us to which this life is only a preparatory school. It is not unreasonable to think it is so—that when this fitful fever is over we may pass out into realms and into a state of being in which the muddle of this strange episode will be resolved. But here we are finite. Here we have no abiding city and all our feelings are conditioned by finite terms. We are rather like the batsman at the wicket. He does not want to get out. When he has made his 50 he strives to make his 100, and when he has made his 100, he is just as anxious to make 200. But it is the knowledge that the innings will end, that

On Living for Ever

every ball may be his last, that gives zest to the game. If he knew that he never could get out, that by an inexorable decree he was to be at the wicket for the rest of his days, he would turn round and knock the stumps down in desperation.

No, Mr. Rutherford, you have mistaken us. We do not want your revelation. The play is worth seeing, though I wish it were more good-humoured and the players a little more friendly; but we do not wish to watch it for ever. We like to know that the curtain will fall and that, a little weary and sleepy, we shall be permitted to go home. We are in no hurry, sir, but we like to know that the curtain is there.

ON INITIALS

A LETTER came to me the other day from a gentleman
of the name of Blodgett, residing in Chicago. I do not,
I regret to say, know Mr. Blodgett, but he has heard
about me and even read my books, and he has a desire
—which I find it difficult to resent—to possess my
autograph. He wants to place it "in the literary
shrine in his library" beside the autographs of "G. K.
Chesterton, J. M. Barrie, A. A. Milne, E. V. Lucas,
Lord Northcliffe," and other deities that he apparently worships in far-away Chicago. I yielded to Mr.
Blodgett's request, for I am not made of the stern
stuff that can turn a deaf ear to flattery. I endeavour
to mortify the pride that Mr. Blodgett's compliment
arouses by reflecting that for one person who wants
my autograph there are one million who would wade
through blood and tears for Charlie Chaplin's, or
Georges Carpentier's, or Mary Pickford's, or the late
Monsieur Landru's, or the eminent Mr. Horatio
Bottomley's. I recalled the scene I saw at Lord's a
few days ago when at the end of an innings as the teams
left the field an enormous crowd rushed forward and
enveloped them like a plague of locusts, each with
an open book in one hand and a pen in the other, and
a prayer on the lips for the autograph of some illustrious player. I reflected that no mob ever pursued me
with these flattering attentions.

But in vain. The agreeable incense goes to my

On Initials

head. A request for my autograph makes me swell with pomp. However hard I try to be humble, I can't do it. The vision of Mr. Blodgett (of Chicago) rises before me. I see him carrying my illustrious autograph about in his breast-pocket and stopping his friends on Michigan Avenue to flaunt my flourishes before their eyes. I see him arriving home in the evening and shouting the glad tidings that my autograph has come to Mrs. Blodgett and the young Blodgetts up the staircase. And I sink to sleep at night with the agreeable vision of my humble signature resting in the "literary shrine" of Mr. Blodgett beside the august name of "Northcliffe."

But I refer to Mr. Blodgett's letter not because of his request, but because of his manner of addressing me. He writes to me as "Reginald S. Thomson, Esq." I cannot deny that my name (for the purpose of this article) is Reginald. I wish I could. What possessed my revered parents—peace to their ashes—to call me Reginald I do not know. Perhaps it was out of respect for the memory of the saintly Heber, whose precocious piety was set before me, with not much success, for my youthful imitation. But whatever its origin, I cannot recall the time when I did not loathe the name of Reginald. I took the earliest opportunity of disowning it, and for fifty years I have passed through the world under the sign of R. S. Thomson. Our English habit of using initials only for our Christian names was a source of solace to me. It enabled me to forget all about Reginald, and to leave the world in darkness about my disgraceful secret. I left it to suppose, if it supposed at all, that

On Initials

behind the R. there lurked nothing more offensive than Robert, or Richard, or, at the worst, Rufus.

A visit to America, however, betrayed the wretched truth to the world. The Americans are as particular about flourishing their front names as we often are about concealing ours. Mr. Herodotus P. Champ would be cut to the quick if you addressed him as Mr. H. P. Champ. He would regard it as a studied affront. And, being a polite people, the Americans take as much pains to unearth the Christian names of their visitors as their visitors take to hide them. Nothing will convince them that we wear initials because we like them. I had no sooner stepped ashore at New York than I was confronted with Mr. Reginald S. Thomson. Wherever I went I was haunted by that objectionable person. He went with me into parlours and on to platforms. He gibed at me in headlines. He mocked at me with his Portland slip and his white spats and his eye-glass. It was not until I had placed the Atlantic between myself and America that I ceased to be shadowed by Reginald. He is still over there, holding me up to ridicule with his insufferable elegances.

No doubt others have suffered in the same way. It would not surprise me to learn that Mr. H. G. Wells is known from Boston to Los Angeles as Mr. Hannibal G. Wells. Nobody in England knows what lurks behind "H. G." Mr. Wells keeps the secret from his closest friends, but I daresay it is babbled all over America, and that there is not an intelligent schoolboy who does not discuss the latest book of Hector G. Wells or H. Gascoigne Wells, or Horatio

On Initials

Gordon Wells, as the case may be. No doubt Mr. Wells has excellent reasons for not publishing his front names to the world. He may dislike them as much as I dislike Reginald. Parents who give us our names immediately we appear in the world are naturally liable to do us an injury. They have, let us say, been stirred by some royal wedding, and call their poor infant "Lascelles" in a fervour of loyalty. And perhaps Lascelles grows up into a fierce Communist who would prefer the L. to stand for Lenin. What is he to do but to take refuge in initials? And since he alone is concerned, why should we pry into the secrets which those initials conceal?

It would be a simple way of relief if our baptismal names were temporary, and each of us chose the names by which he desired to be known on coming of age. Then they would fit us more happily than Reginald fits me or Hannibal—if it is Hannibal— fits Mr. Wells.

PLANTING A SPINNEY

THE idea of planting a spinney arose out of the necessity of finding a name for the cottage. It is difficult to find a name for anything, from a baby to a book, but it is most difficult of all to find a name for a house. At least so we found it. Jane wanted "The Knoll," and somebody else, with a taste for Hardy, wanted "The Knap," and someone else, as a tribute to Meredith (and in view of the fact that the upland we had built on was a famous place for skylarks), wanted "Lark Uprising" (what would the postman have thought?), and another wanted "Windy Gap," and so on, and amid the multitude of suggestions the cottage seemed as though it would lose its youth and grow old without any name at all.

Then one day someone said "The Spinney," and in sheer desperation everyone else said, "Why, of course, 'The Spinney.' Perfect. The very thing." The only objection that was made was that there was no spinney. But a good name could not be sacrificed to so negligible a consideration. Moreover, what had we been about to forget to plant so desirable a thing as a spinney? There, below the house, just out of the line of view so as not to blot out the landscape of four counties, was the very spot, and in the garden there were plenty of trees, pine, spruce, chestnut, beech, and lime of twelve or fifteen years' growth ready to hand. It would have been safer and simpler to have set young saplings, but that would not have

Planting a Spinney

satisfied the elders. It would have been starting a spinney for another generation to enjoy, and we wanted a spinney that we could sit under ourselves.

If you plant saplings, I think you ought to do it in your youth so that you and the trees can grow to maturity and age together. I often regret that I did not plant an acorn from that glorious tree, the Queen Elizabeth's oak at Chenies, when I was young. It would have been a stalwart fellow by this time with a comfortable shade on summer days. But now, no, I should be too heavily handicapped in the race, and the young oak just starting on its prodigious career would mock my little span. One ought not, of course, to be sentimental over such things, but if you love trees you cannot help it. Witness that story in Tacitus of the noble Roman who owned the garden of Lucullus and who, being sentenced to be burned in his garden, asked permission the night before his execution to go and choose the place for the funeral pyre in order that the flames which consumed him should spare the trees he loved. That is a fine legend by which to be remembered for two thousand years.

I was told the other day a pleasant fact about Sir Henry Campbell-Bannerman which will endear him still more to some and make him appear, perhaps, absurd to others. When he went from London to his estate of Belmont in Scotland, it was his practice to walk round his park and take off his hat to the trees he loved most. If Sir Henry had been given to irony, it might be supposed that the gesture was intended as a compliment on the company he had left behind at Westminster. "The more I see of men,"

Planting a Spinney

he might have meant, adapting Pascal's famous phrase, "the better I like trees." But I do not fancy there was any anger with men in his greeting. There was nothing of the misanthrope in that shrewd and companionable man. He was a good hater, and had as acute a sense of character as any man of his time. He knew a crook or a humbug by instinct, and anything fraudulent or shoddy withered in his presence; but an honest, plain man was always at home with him.

He saluted his favourite trees in the spirit in which Xerxes, when passing with his army through Lydia, decorated with golden ornaments a plane-tree of extraordinary beauty, and left a warrior from the Immortal Band to be its special guard, as you may read in Herodotus. He saluted them because he loved them, and no one who has the spirit of the woodlands in him will think the action odd or even fanciful. It has never occurred to me to go about the woods taking off my hat to the kings of the forest, but that only shows that I have less imagination and less chivalry than he had. I am not sure I shall not do so in future. It is the least courtesy I can offer them for all the pleasure they have given me in life, and the action will seem reasonable enough to anyone who has witnessed those wonderful experiments of Professor Bhose which reveal the inner life of the tree with such thrilling suggestions of consciousness and emotion.

It is not possible to live much among trees without experiencing a subtle sense of comradeship with them. Our intimacy may not go so far as that of Giles Winterbourn, in *The Woodlanders*, who could

Planting a Spinney

tell what sort of trees he was passing in the dark by the sound of the wind in the branches—but without that erudition it can create an affection almost personal, not unlike that we feel for those quiet companions of whom we have not thought much, perhaps, until we find that their simple constancy and friendliness had made the atmosphere and sunshine in which we moved.

I confess that when I walk through the woods that crown the hills behind the cottage, and see the great boles of the noblest of the beeches marked for felling, I feel very much as when I hear bad news of an old friend. That those glorious fellows, whom I have seen clothing themselves with green in the spring and with gold in the autumn, should be brought low and split into fragments to make chairs and tables seems a sacrilege. It is an unpractical sentiment, of course, and I daresay if I owned the trees I should cut them down too. So I am glad I don't own them, and can just love them and lament them.

I should, however, find it hard to cut down beech-trees of all trees, for after many affairs of the heart with trees, my affections have settled finally on them as the pride of our English woodlands. With what stateliness they spring from the ground, how noble their shade, how exquisite the green of their leaves in spring, how rich the gold of autumn, what a glowing carpet they spread for us in winter! If I go to Epping Forest it is to see the grand patriarchs of the tribe who are gathered together in solemn conclave in Monk's Wood, and if I place Buckinghamshire high among the counties, it is because there you will find a more abundant wealth of beeches than anywhere else in the land.

But I am no narrow sectarian about trees. If I put the beech first, I worship at many shrines. When I go to Chenies it is to pay my devotions to the Duke of Bedford's oaks, and especially the aforesaid Queen Elizabeth's oak, which still strews the greensward with acorns, though in its ancient trunk, hollowed by the centuries, you could seat a tolerably large tea-party. And who would go to Shere without a visit to those stalwart Spanish chestnuts that are the glory of the Duke of Northumberland's park? It is worth a journey to Salisbury, not merely to see the spire and Stonehenge, but to make the acquaintance of those magnificent cedars in Wilton Park. There is an elm at Nuneham that I go to see much as I go to see a venerable relative, and there is a wonderful yew-tree in the churchyard of Tidworth in Surrey that is better worth a pilgrimage than many a cathedral.

But to return to the spinney. We began our adventure a year ago, between the months of November and February, which are the limits within which transplanting can be done. A dozen spruce, two pines, a sycamore and two limes, all standing ten to a dozen feet in their boots, so to speak, were, with enormous gruntings, heavings and perspirations, borne to the chosen spot, and there placed in new-dug holes, earthed up, wired in position, and left to weather the storms. The handy-man shook his head over the operation—"didn't know but what they warn't too big to shift, but happen some on 'em would live." All through the spring and summer I watched

Planting a Spinney

those trees struggling for life, like a doctor walking the wards of a hospital and feeling the pulses of his patients. Month by month the spruces flickered on. The fairest of them all was the first to give up the ghost definitely, and then three others followed. It was August before any shoots of new foliage began to appear, and then one by one the remainder put forth tiny buds of life, the last sending out his faint signal of spring as late as October. "Ain't done so bad," said the handy-man, scratching his head to help him to a right judgment.

To-day with more heavings and gruntings the handy-man and I have transplanted another bunch of pines a good fifteen feet in height to the spinney, and for months to come I shall walk the wood again to catch signs of life in my new patients. Meanwhile, in order to provide for the future, we have planted young saplings among the big trees, and altogether my spinney, I think, makes a handsome show. I have just had a walk along the lane below to view it as a stranger might, and, speaking as a stranger, I remarked to myself that that was a nice little spinney beside the cottage on the hill, and when I came to the gate I, still as a stranger, was struck by the appropriateness of the name. I think that that spinney will be my memorial to the countryside, and I want no better. There is no pleasanter thing to be remembered by than trees. They are better than battles or books, for they do not record our passions, our ambitions, or our contentions. They record only that we once passed this way and loved the friendliness of the woods.

ON WEARING AN EYEGLASS

"ROUGHLY speaking," says a writer in a recent issue of the *New Statesman*, "no man using or wearing a monocle should be appointed to any public post in the United States. Believe me, nothing short of his fine simplicity and intellectual integrity would have enabled Mr. William Archer to 'get away with it.'" The warning occurs in an admirable article dealing with the disastrous way in which official England is usually represented in America. It is a subject of first importance, on which I am in entire agreement with the writer, and about which I could say much from personal knowledge. But the eyeglass will serve. You can see the whole landscape surveyed by the writer through the Englishman's eyeglass.

And, first, let me clear away the suggestion about my good friend William Archer. It is true he carries an eyeglass, and I have seen him on occasion use it to examine documents. But he does not *wear* an eyeglass, and he does wear spectacles. Neither in fact nor in spirit can he be included in the ranks of the Eyeglass Englishman. Nor, indeed, can all those who do wear an eyeglass be included in that category. I have known men who succeeded in wearing an eyeglass without offence. I have even known a lady who wore one so naturally and with such a suggestion of unconsciousness that you yourself were almost unconscious that she wore it.

On Wearing an Eyeglass

But, generally speaking, an eyeglass is an ostentation. It is an ostentation because it is so much more natural, easy and unaffected to wear spectacles, which serve precisely the same uses. You put a pair of spectacles on your nose and forget all about them. And the world forgets all about them. You cannot do that with an eyeglass. The world cannot do that with an eyeglass. Spectacles convey no implications, carry no comment; but an eyeglass is as declaratory as a Union Jack. It is a public announcement of ourselves. It is an intimation to the world that we have arrived. And the world takes note of the fact. When it thinks of Mr. Austen Chamberlain, it thinks of an eyeglass as inevitably as when it thinks of Nelson it thinks of an armless sleeve, or when it thinks of Richard III. it thinks of a hump-back. An eyeglass is as troublesome as a feverish baby. It is an occupation. It is almost a career. It is always dropping out and being reaffixed with an ugly contortion of the muscles of the eye-socket. And if, by long practice, it is kept in position without contortion, you are insensibly kept wondering how the feat is performed and waiting for the laws of Nature to operate.

In a word, a monocle calls attention to itself. It is a calculated affectation. It is an advertisement that we are someone in particular, and that we expect to be observed. It is as much a symbol of class consciousness as the red tie of the Socialist, and it is much less pleasing, for the red tie is an assertion of human equality, while the monocle sets up a claim to social exclusiveness. The wearer of the red tie wants everybody to wear red ties. The more red ties

On Wearing an Eyeglass

he sees, the happier he feels. If everybody wore red ties it would be very heaven. Surely the millennium is at hand, he would say. He would feel the spasm that Hyndman felt when he noticed that all the porters of a certain station were wearing red ties. "See," he said to John Burns, "see the red ties! the social revolution is on the march." "Nothing of the sort," said Burns. "It's a part of the station uniform." Hyndman's face fell, for he did really want to see everybody wearing the same coloured tie as himself. But if one morning Lord Dundreary (late of the Guards) saw the whole of Piccadilly bursting out into monocles, every policeman wearing a monocle, and every cabman wearing a monocle, and everybody in the buses wearing a monocle, he would feel that the pillars of the firmament were tumbling down. He would take off his monocle and grind it under his heel. He must belong to an exclusive set or cease to find life livable.

The philosophy of the eyeglass is explained in the familiar story of Disraeli and Chamberlain. When the famous Israelite, who was an artifice from the curl plastered on his forehead to the sole of his foot, saw through his eyeglass the terrible Radical Mayor of Birmingham enter the House for the first time, he turned to his neighbour and said: "He wears his eyeglass *like a gentleman*." He was satisfied. There was no reason to fear the Mayor of Birmingham. He was "one of us." No one would say that So-and-So "wears his spectacles like a gentleman" any more than he would say that he "wears his hat" (or his boots) "like a gentleman." What Disraeli meant was

On Wearing an Eyeglass

that Chamberlain could do an exceptional thing with the air of one who was doing an ordinary thing. He knew how to be conspicuous without being unhappy. He wore the badge of the superior person as if he had forgotten it was there. He wore it as though Nature had decorated him at birth with the Order of the Eyeglass. He was a Perfect Gentleman.

There is nothing wrong in being a Perfect Gentleman. It is a very proper ambition; but we ought not to label ourselves Perfect Gentlemen. We ought to be content to leave the world to discover that we are Perfect Gentlemen, and not proclaim the fact by means of a pane of glass hung perilously in the right eye. For, according to the practice of the best circles, it should always be in the right eye. The left eye may be as blind as a bat, but it would never do to wear a pane of glass there. If you do that you do not know the first law of the Cult of the Eyeglass. None of the best people wear the monocle in the left eye. It is like eating peas with your knife, or tucking your serviette in at your collar, as the Germans (who are most Imperfect Gentlemen) do, instead of wearing it on your knees, where it will not get in the way of anything that happens to fall.

It is impossible to think of greatness in the terms of the eyeglass. Shakespeare himself could hardly survive so limiting and belittling a circumstance. Try to think of Milton, in the days before blindness had come upon him, sitting at Cromwell's elbow with an eyeglass in his right eye. Imagine Gladstone or Newman wearing eyeglasses. The mind rejects the image as a sort of sacrilege. Indeed one may almost say that

On Wearing an Eyeglass

the measure of greatness is the extent of the humiliation which an eyeglass would inflict upon the subject. And, yet again—so dangerous is it to generalise—there are rare cases in which an eyeglass seems the fitting property of the man. Joseph Conrad was such a case. There was in him a haughty aloofness from the drama that he observed with such cold and dispassionate understanding that his eyeglass had a certain significance that gave it warrant. He did not wear it "like a gentleman." He wore it like a being of another creation.

I do not know whether we invented the monocle, nor do I know whether it is a peculiarly English institution; I fancy it is. In any case, it is the universal attribute of the stage Englishman abroad, and in America, where an eyeglass would be an offence against the unwritten law of the republic, it symbolises all those manners of the superior person whose export abroad, and especially to the United States, does our interests much harm. The warning of the writer in the *New Statesman* is badly needed. Let us keep the Eyeglass Englishman (whether he wears an eyeglass or not) at home, where we are used to him, and where he can do no mischief. After all, he does not represent us. He is only one in ten thousand of us. Why should he be chosen to make us misunderstood by people who dislike the idea of social caste and all its appurtenances?

A MAN AND HIS WATCH

I SUPPOSE most people recognised something of themselves in the story, reported in the papers the other day, about the man and his watch. He was hurrying to the station when it occurred to him that he had not got his watch on. So he took his watch out of his pocket to see if he had time to run home and get it. I do not know how the affair continued; but I like to think of him hurrying back, bursting into his house, bouncing upstairs, feeling under his pillow for the watch, finding it was not there, and creating a fine hubbub in his family, before his little daughter remarks that it is in his pocket. And of course he misses the train. We have all done this sort of thing. A very grave and responsible man who sat in Parliament for many years told me that he went up to his bedroom one evening to change into evening-dress. And at the stage of undressing at which the ceremony of winding up his watch usually occurred, he wound it up, put it under his pillow—and got into bed. Happily, before he had fallen asleep he remembered that he had come up, not to undress for bed, but to dress for dinner.

I had an absurd experience of the kind myself not long ago. As everyone knows, there are two tube-stations at Oxford Circus, connected underground. I went down the lift at one station intending to catch a train somewhere, and walked along the subway

A Man and His Watch

until I came to a lift, into which a crowd of people were hurrying. I suppose my mind was occupied with some affair, and the mere habit of joining any crowd that is going into any lift swept me in on the tide. The ticket-collector was too busy to check my ticket, and I duly found myself out in the street again at the place from which I had started before I realised what I had done. I have the less hesitation in making this confession because few of us can have failed to have some experience of the sort. Most of our actions are as automatic as the functions of walking, or breathing, or masticating our food. They have become so habitual that we do not have to think about doing them. They perform themselves, as it were, without our help.

If it is your custom to lock up at night and put out the lights, you do so quite mechanically, and if, having locked the sitting-room door and reached the foot of the stairs, your mind chances to wake up and inquire: "Now did you put the lights out?" and sends you back to make sure, you never fail to find that the action has performed itself without any conscious effort on your part. It used to be no uncommon thing for my family to find the front-door securely bolted in broad daylight. I was in those days always the last home at night, and, having opened and closed the door, it was my custom to stoop down and bolt it. If by chance I came in during the morning or afternoon the process was faithfully performed. The habit of bolting the door had become a part of the habit of unlocking it, and it needed a conscious effort of the mind to break the sequence. Or to take

A Man and His Watch

another example, anybody can walk asleep down his own stairs quite safely, but if he woke up at the head of the stairs in the dark and began to think how the stairs went on and how many there were, he would not be able to get down them without feeling his way like a blind man.

And most of us, I suppose, know how easy it is to forget the most familiar name when the mind wakes up and urgently asks for it. You are talking, let us say, to Blessington when up comes Whorlow. You know Whorlow as well as you know your own shadow, and if you met him in the street in the ordinary way his name would be on your tongue as naturally as your own. But now your mind interferes. It demands Whorlow's name for the purposes of introduction on the spot—instantly. The passive habit of thinking Whorlow when you see Whorlow vanishes. Your active thought becomes engaged. It rushes round in search of his name, and cannot find it, and you end by mumbling something unintelligible. And probably Whorlow, who is a little sensitive about his name, feels that you have deliberately slighted him.

It is not difficult to credit the stories of the people who forget their own names or their own telephone number. These things have been committed to the automatic workings of the mind. Our active thought is not concerned with them, and when we consciously think about them they escape. As Samuel Butler says, we don't know a thing until we have ceased to know that we know it. If we ask ourselves whether we know it we are on the way to being lost. He takes the case of the accomplished pianist who rattles off

A Man and His Watch

a nocturne of Chopin or an impromptu of Schubert without a check or a mistake. The habit of the thing acquired by infinite practice carries him on like the wind. But let him be stopped in mid-flight, as it were, and then begin to think about the notes, and he will flounder and hesitate until the current of habit seizes him again and sweeps him to the close. Anyone can provide illustrations out of his own experience. I can spell Philippi as well as most if I take it at a rush, but if I begin by asking myself how to spell it, I fancy I should get entangled in the "l's" and "p's."

In the case of the man and his watch, we see this conflict of the active and passive mind in its most elementary form. His conscious thought is that he has forgotten his watch and that there is little time to spare to get it. Is there enough time? In comes habit and takes his watch out of his pocket to tell him how long it is before the train starts. The action is so automatic that he does not associate it with the subject of his disquietude. And there he stands, looking at his watch to see if he has time to go home and get it—a perpetual joke which we can all enjoy, none the less, perhaps all the more, because we suspect that we all stand there with him.

YOUTH AND OLD AGE

"THE Abbé, in spite of his fifty-eight years . . ."
I was reading a story of De Maupassant in a railway-
train, when this bitter reflection on my age pulled me
up with a slight shock. I was on my way to a cricket-
match—my annual cricket-match; my team against
the village team—and this suggestion that I was an
obsolescent old fellow cast a momentary shadow
over my spirit. But I remembered that De Maupassant died in the thirties or early forties and that he
could not be expected to know that fifty-eight is
about the time when a man ought to be getting his
second wind.

It is the habit of youth to antedate old age in this
offensive way. Jane Austen, who died, I think, when
she was under forty, was accustomed in her twenties
to write of people who had passed forty as if they had
come out of the Ark, and Addison speaks in his essay
on the "Widows' Club" of a man of sixty as if the
fact was sufficient to show that he was in the last
stages of senile decay. I had the curiosity to look up
Addison's age at his death and found it was forty-six.
It gave me a curious sensation to discover that that
grave and elderly spirit had died when he was twelve
years my junior. He had always seemed to me so much
older than I could ever hope to be that it had never
occurred to me to measure my years with his.

Youth and Old Age

It is one of the humbling experiences we have as we grow older to find that, in years, we have left behind so many of those who filled the world with the sound of their name without having ourselves yet done anything to boast about. Alexander only lived half my lifetime; Shelley and Keats when they died were young enough to be the sons of a man of fifty-eight; Napoleon was the first man in Europe at twenty-seven and had reached Waterloo at forty-six; all the vast world of Shakespeare had been created when he was in the early forties; the younger Pitt was Prime Minister twenty years and died at an age when Mr. Lloyd George was still a private member. And so on.

The explanation, I suppose, is that modern conditions have put old age off ten or twenty years. When Jane Austen wrote of elderly men of forty she did so because they were elderly men at forty. What with their weakness for port wine—both Addison and Pitt were notorious for the amount of liquor they carried —and the rudimentary knowledge of disease and its causes, life was a much briefer affair than it is now. Whatever grievance we may have against the age of science, it has made our days long in the land, and what is more important, it has made them healthier. The average man of sixty to-day is, counting age in real values, younger than the average man of fifty in the eighteenth century. That is no doubt one of the reasons why youth does not cut quite such a dash in the world as it did when Napoleon was the first soldier in Europe at twenty-seven, and Pitt the first states-man in Europe at twenty-six. The old fellows go on

Youth and Old Age

living and insisting on being young and keeping their jobs.

They even go on playing cricket and watching cricket. When I got on the village playground, I found among the spectators a gay old gentleman of ninety-three, of whom I have written before in these articles, who never misses a match, and who looks on a man of fifty-eight as a person who has hardly yet come to years of discretion. His genial greeting blew away the slight shadow cast over me by Maupassant's unkind cut, and "in spite of my fifty-eight years" I succeeded in giving the scorer a bit of trouble, so much so that I thought it worth while when I was out to go and look over his shoulder at the nice little procession of "ones" and "twos" that followed my name. I should have liked Jane Austen and Maupassant and Addison to have looked over the scorer's shoulder with me. They would have changed their tune about old fellows of fifty-eight.

THE GOLDEN AGE

I SEE that Dean Inge has been lamenting that he did not live a couple of generations ago. He seems to think that the world was a much more desirable place then, that it has been going to the dogs ever since, and that the only comfortable thought that we can cultivate in this degenerate time is that we shall soon be out of it. Assuming for the moment that the world was a happier place fifty or sixty years ago, I doubt whether it follows that the Dean would have been happier in it than he is in our world to-day. The measure of personal happiness is fortunately not dependent on external circumstances. It is affected by them, of course. Most of us are more agreeable people when we have dined than when we are hungry, when we have slept well than when we have not slept at all, when our horse or our party has won than when it has lost, when things go right than when things go wrong. No philosophy is an anodyne for the tooth-ache, and the east wind plays havoc with the feelings of the best of us. In these and a thousand other ways we are the sport of circumstance, but in this respect we are no better and no worse off than our forbears fifty years ago or five hundred years ago, or than our descendants will be fifty or five hundred years hence.

But our essential happiness or unhappiness is independent of these things. It is a quality of character.

The Golden Age

It may have a physical basis. Our happiness, said the French lady to Boswell, depends upon the circulation of the blood. It may equally depend on our nervous constitution or the functioning of our organs. I cannot doubt that the Carlyles would have been happier people if they had had better digestions. They lived in that period which is held up to us as the time when it was good to be alive, but it is doubtful whether two more miserable people than they were are to be found on earth to-day, and Carlyle himself damned his own time even more bitterly than the Dean damns this. He would have damned any time in which he had the misfortune to live, for life would always have been a sorrowful affair to him. It was his habit of mind. And the world for each of us is what the mind makes it.

> The mind is its own place, and in itself
> Can make a heaven of hell, a hell of heaven.

In short, whether life is a comedy or a tragedy or just a humdrum affair that cannot be called either, does not depend upon the time in which we happen to live, for it is all these things at all times. It depends upon our point of view. I fancy Little Tich would have found the world as amusing as a country fair if he had lived in the Rome of Caligula, and I am sure that Carlyle would have found it as sad as a funeral if he had lived in the Garden of Eden. There is no question of merit or virtue in the matter. If there is, it is not the meritorious or the virtuous who are usually the most happy. It is they who take life lightly and indifferently who get the most fun out of it. I doubt whether there was ever a more odious monster

The Golden Age

on earth than Sulla, whose savageries and debaucheries made him not so much a man as a satyr. Yet, except for the hideous disease from which he died, there can hardly ever have been a more fortunate man or one who found the world, in a gross sense, a more amusing place. Even when his corpse was burned with the accustomed solemnities, the wind blew and the rain fell in perfect time and sequence, "so that," as Plutarch says, "his good fortune was firm even to the last, and did as it were officiate at his funeral." Dean Swift cursed the day he was born, though he lived in the relatively comfortable time of Queen Anne, and being the man he was, he would have cursed the day he was born no matter what period of history he had lived in. He carried an unhappy world in the terrific gloom of his own mind.

Indeed, if we want to play with the idea of how we might have been happy, it is not the thought of living in other times that will satisfy us, but the thought of living other men's lives. If I had the privilege of antedating my birth, I would not bother about the period, but would choose very carefully my personality. Among the ancients I should select to be Herodotus, whose immortal work is saturated with the sunshine of as delighted a spirit as ever walked the earth. And among the moderns I would choose with equal confidence to live the life of Macaulay. It is true that he wept very copiously. I have amused myself sometimes in reading his "Life," by collating the occasions on which he was in tears. He could have said with Michelet, "Le don que Saint Louis demande et n'obtient pas, je l'eus 'Le don des larmes.'" Novels and

The Golden Age

poetry were bedewed with his tears. He wept whenever he was reminded of the sister he had lost, when he visited his old home in Bloomsbury, when he said "Hail!" and when he said "Farewell!" when friends fell away, and when foes, like Peel, passed into silence. But, in spite of his overcharged affection, what a rich, full, joyous life it was! What zest, what kindliness, what noble feeling, what fine living! I put Macaulay lower in the scale of literature than I once did, but in the scale of humanity there is none higher.

There never was a golden age in which happiness was the universal portion, nor one in which it was denied to those who had the gift within. It is a personal affair, not an affair of time, place or condition, and if we are sad, it is idle to lament that we were not born in days when we could have been merry. Sancho Panza is happy in any age, and Don Quixote is always sorrowful.

THE TOP OF THE LADDER

I suppose that if we had been asked, any time during the first twenty years of this century, who was the most enviable of living men, Caruso would, in the popular opinion, have had the first place. He had out-soared challenge. He was the idol of both hemispheres. He earned the income of a prince, and he earned it in the most pleasurable of all ways by giving pleasure to others and winning fame for himself. Yet he declared himself to be "often the unhappiest of men." And his unhappiness was that worst form of unhappiness, the canker of success. "When I was unknown," he said, "I sang like a bird, careless, without thought of nerves. But I am bending to-day beneath the weight of renown which cannot increase, but which the least vocal mishap may compromise. That is why I am often the unhappiest of men."

It is the penalty exacted by success. The top of the ladder is a desirable place, and we all like to get there, but having got there we find that the foothold is precarious and that the drop is deep. A fall from the lower rungs of the ladder does us no harm. We can pick ourselves up and start again with a good heart, and without much hurt to our self-esteem. We may get higher, and in any case we shall not fall lower. And in the meantime there is the joy of "getting there" to spur us on. We are happy in the pursuit of happiness. There it dwells at the top rung of the ladder and if only we can reach it all our yearnings will be satisfied and we shall enter into a seraphic peace of possession that will be undisturbed. And having got there we find that all the fun was in the climbing, and that the prize is a fleeting rainbow. There is no way farther up and the way down is easy. The crowd shouts its applause from below, but Martinelli is coming up behind and will shove Caruso over the top.

But Caruso, like Nelson, had the good fortune not to outlive his triumph. "Go at your zenith" was Nelson's maxim, and it is difficult to read the story of his deliberate exposure of himself at Trafalgar without concluding that he sought death. It was a stroke of his emotional and decisive genius, and it left him immortally at the top of the ladder. Had Wellington died at Waterloo he would have been there with him, instead of being remembered as a grumpy old gentleman who blocked the path and said "damn," and had his windows broken by the mob.

It is asking for trouble to expect a permanent dwelling-place at the top of the ladder, and to pin one's happiness to such an uncertain tenure. Life is a great comedian, and plays merciless practical jokes with its most august victims. It thrust the young Corsican up to a height of power unparalleled in the history of the world and then left him to eat his heart out on a bit of rock in a remote ocean, growing prematurely old and fat and diseased. But Napoleon's penalty was light compared with that of the Kaiser, who must surely hold the record for all time as the

The Top of the Ladder

sport of the gods. Napoleon at least knew what a fickle thing success was. Starting with nothing, he had won the world, and to his cynical and *realpolitik* mind there was nothing surprising in his loss of what he had won.

But the Kaiser had never had the salutary teaching of experience. He was born at the top of the ladder, and could conceive of no existence away from that dizzy eminence; he really believed that he belonged to a semi-divine order, and if we had had the misfortune to be born in his circumstances most of us would have had the same illusion. Now, after such splendour of power as Louis XIV. himself never enjoyed, he is cast aside like an old shoe, disowned by his people, repudiated by his relatives, his empire shrunk to the dimensions of a Dutch garden, and he himself become, to all appearances, of no more significance than if he were an Italian organ-grinder or blew the trombone in a German band. He must surely have had a larger measure than any man in history of what Chaucer calls the heaviest of all afflictions:

> For of fortune's sharp adversitee,
> The worst kind of infortune is this,
> A man to have ben in prosperitee
> And it remembren when it passèd is.

"And it remembren when it passèd is." It was that bitterness which Caruso feared even when he was at the top of the ladder. It is that bitterness which is about all that life has left to the negligible exile in Holland.

IN a matter of taste we cannot expect a decisive verdict, and it is probable therefore that the discussion which is proceeding in the Press as to whether we are more handsome than our forefathers will leave this interesting problem unsettled. "Of course men are growing more handsome," says Sir William Orpen, the painter. "Of course men are not growing more handsome," says Professor Geddes, the sociologist. Between the two views comes that of Professor Keith, the anthropologist, who says simply that faces are changing, whether for better or worse he does not venture an opinion.

I have no doubt that Professor Geddes has got his eye on the Greeks. He usually has. And if we bring the ancient Greeks into the competition I do not see how the verdict can go against him. The memorials they have left of the human face and form are still the accepted standard of beauty. The highest praise that the idolaters of that young Apollo, Carpentier, can give him is that he is like a Greek god. And the Romans were handsome fellows, too. Judging from the most famous and most authentic bust of Cæsar , that great man had a face of extraordinary intellectual beauty. If you were to put, let us say, a bust of Mr. Winston Churchill beside that of Cæsar, you would not be disposed to say that we had achieved much in the way of growing handsome in the course of two thousand years. There were ugly fellows then, of course, as there are ugly fellows now. Sulla, with his blotched and satyr face, was as unpleasant in appearance as he was in character, and the great Socrates was no thing of beauty. But in comparing ourselves with the past we must compare best with best.

And if we leave the ancient world and come down to a time of which we have authentic records in portraiture, the evidence is still with Geddes. You would have to stand a long time in the Strand before you saw coming along its populous pavements a face of such sublimity as that of Dante, and I fancy that if Beatrice appeared in a ball-room in Belgravia she would not lack suitors for a dance. Take the men that Dürer and Holbein painted four hundred years ago. It will be hard to match the exquisite sensitiveness and enlightenment that live in the face of Erasmus, or the dignity and noble austerity of Bellini's portrait of the great Doge Loredano, which you may see in the National Gallery. Is there a face comparable with it in the House of Commons to-day? And what of that wonderful face of the Bishop in the Ansidei Madonna of Raphael which you may also see in the National Gallery?

And coming down a century or so later, and to another land, have we much ground for thinking we of to-day are more handsome than Velasquez' Spaniards? Put Sir William Orpen's portraits of the modern English into competition with Velasquez' portraits of the Spaniards of three hundred years

On Faces—Past and Present

ago, and you will feel you have passed to a lower plane of beauty. You may say that it is unfair to compare a supreme artist with a merely clever technician; but the material they have worked on is the faces they have seen about them, and the faces of Velasquez live in the memory like a sonnet of Keats and the faces of Orpen leave no impression behind. Where will the much-praised "Chef" be beside the solemn beauty of Velasquez' "Menippus" three hundred years hence? Where will it be even beside the "Tailor" of Moroni, to which it offers so commonplace a challenge?

Or take our own country. While Velasquez was painting the princes and beggars of Spain, Vandyck was painting the princes and nobles of our own Court. By comparison with the faces of Velasquez, the faces of Vandyck are shallow and sentimental; but no one will deny that they are handsome faces. No one will deny, for example, that Charles I. was as handsome as any king we have had in the last century. And I suppose, judging by the records of the young Milton, it would be difficult to find in all our millions to-day a face of equal beauty to his.

I am not suggesting by all this that, so far from growing more handsome, we are growing less handsome. The probability is that the proportion of handsome faces remains about the same in all generations. But no doubt time changes the lines both of face and form. I am told that the armour in the Tower worn by the warriors of the past would be too tight a fit for the average well-developed man of to-day, and I suppose our jaws have narrowed, for the skulls of

ancient peoples are remarkable for the evenness of
the teeth, while to-day the bulk of us have more teeth
than we have room for, and have to have some out
or carry them sideways. Changes like these are due
to changed conditions—softer foods, more knowledge
of the body and its needs, and so on. Women, for
example, are taller than they were a few generations
ago when convention denied them the muscular
exercises of to-day. The coming of the bicycle was
their real emancipation. It abolished the long skirt,
gave them the freedom of their limbs, and in the
end the freedom of their minds. They are not more
beautiful than their grandmothers were, but they
are different. Perhaps they are better.

IN PRAISE OF MAIDEN AUNTS

I HAVE received a rebuke from a lady at Cardiff, that, though unmerited, calls for respectful attention. In an article written during the crisis in Anglo-French relations, I said that the visits of English Ministers to M. Poincaré made as little impression on him as a visit from his maiden aunt would do. My correspondent takes the illustration as an affront to maiden aunts. "Is a maiden aunt in your opinion the most contemptible thing on earth?" she demands. "If you would say 'Yes,' please open your eyes and think again. If you would say 'No,' will you kindly help us to scotch this vulgar lie by refraining from using this irrelevant metaphor?"

I offer my correspondent and the whole company of maiden aunts a sincere assurance that in taking their names in vain I had no intention to imply a contempt which I certainly did not feel, and which, if I had felt, would have been dishonouring not to them but to me. I wanted to emphasise the disregard of M. Poincaré for the views of the British Government, and chose an illustration which I thought effective. I assumed that however much M. Poincaré loved his maiden aunt (if he has a maiden aunt) he did not act on her advice in state affairs. I still hold that view. I shall give his maiden aunt the credit of thinking that if he followed her opinion he would act with much more wisdom than he has shown. That, I admit, was not in my mind when I wrote, and I will

In Praise of Maiden Aunts

not advance it now as a means of dodging my correspondent's arrow. But while I confess that I thought that maiden aunts were not the persons that prime ministers usually consulted on high politics, I did not mean that they were contemptible or negligible on that account. Maiden aunts, I rejoice to say, have happier and cleaner affairs to occupy them than politics.

Take the most illustrious of all maiden aunts, the dear, lovable, unforgettable Betsy Trotwood. I have had many affairs of the heart in fiction, from Rosalind to Tess, but I do not think that there is any woman who lives in books who ever won my affection more securely and uninterruptedly than Miss Trotwood. It is a pleasure merely to write her name. It must be nearly fifty years since I made that amazing journey with David Copperfield on the Dover road, but I still remember the first meeting with Aunt Betsy as I remember no other adventure in life. David was at his last gasp and I was at my last gasp with him. We could bear no more. And then, looking over the gate—the best-known gate in literature except that "wicket-gate" of another immortal journey—we saw that radiant woman appear with her handkerchief tied over her cap, her gardening gloves on, and her pruning knife in her hand, and there followed that thrilling welcome, the memory of which sweeps over the mind like a wave of glory.

I am told that the boys of to-day do not make that journey on the Dover road, and do not know what it is to feel Aunt Betsy collar them and take them into the parlour and dose them, and bath them and

In Praise of Maiden Aunts

put their tired limbs to bed. Unhappy boys! What a bare, disinherited life is theirs! I would not sacrifice Betsy Trotwood for any memory I have, or the Dover road that brought me to her for any golden road to Samarkand. But I do not recall that Betsy Trotwood cared twopence about politics, or ever mentioned them. She had more serious interests. There were the donkeys to keep at bay, there was Mr. Dick's great mind, "as sharp as a surgeon's lancet," to inquire into, there was her garden, and there was her nephew.

What would David have done without that sublime woman? What would any nephews and nieces do if there were no maiden aunts? Betsy Trotwood was the perfect type and pattern of all the tribe. "There was an inflexibility in her face, in her voice, in her gait and carriage." Listen to the fly-driver of whom David and I inquired the way:

"Trotwood?" said he. "Let me see. I know the name too. Old lady?"

"Yes," I said, "rather."

"Pretty stiff in the back?" said he, making himself upright.

"Yes," I said. "I should think it very likely."

"Carries a bag?" said he, "bag with a good deal of room in it: is gruffish and comes down on you sharp? . . . My opinion is, she won't stand anything, so here's a penny for you."

Admirable fly-driver! But you were mistaken. The outside of our maiden aunts is apt to be roughish, but, like Gunga Din, they are "white, clear white inside." They come down on you sharp, but they have hearts of gold. They are not maiden aunts because they could not be anything else, or are inferior to their sisters, or have less of the milk of human kindness. They have had their romances and put them by,

In Praise of Maiden Aunts

suffered their bereavements, and learned to turn a brave, even harsh, face to the world; but where shall we find such a welcome from the Dover roads of life as they give us, where such a wealth of disinterested affection, where such treasured memories of our thoughtless selves? How many of us have had such a maiden aunt as Betsy Trotwood, a little stiff in the back, as the fly-driver said, a little severe in face and manner perhaps, a bit of a martinet about taking our physic, keeping out of mischief, and things like that, but withal a boundless ocean of affection, a person who had no use for her own birthdays but never forgot ours, who took us to our first play and showed us over the Tower, and was ready to fetch and carry for us till she dropped. Compare them with bachelor uncles. Here and there you may find a brilliant exception, like the uncle in *The Golden Age*, who went away in an auriferous shower, or Macaulay, who must have been the most gorgeous uncle in history; but they are few, and only reveal the general poverty of the tribe, whereas maiden aunts . . .

No, madam, heaven forbid that I should speak disrespectfully of maiden aunts. By the great name of Betsy Trotwood, I swear I am guiltless of such base ingratitude.

．　　．　　．　　．　　．　　．

Do not remind me, dear reader, that Betsy Trotwood was not a maiden aunt. Let us respect her secret which her creator ought never to have disclosed, and remember her as the chief ornament of the goodly company to which she spiritually belonged.

OCTOBER DAYS

JUST below me on the hillside is a forty-acre field
that slopes gently down to the valley. Last year it
was ploughed by a motor-tractor: this year I rejoice
to say it is being ploughed in the old way, as it has
been ploughed for a thousand years. I suppose we
ought to be grateful for the motor-tractor and the
steam-digger that in cheapening production cheapen
our food, but I am glad that the farmer below me has
returned to the ancient way. When the machine comes
in, the poetry goes out, and though poetry has no
place in the farmer's ledger it is pleasant to find that
he has sound reasons for reverting to the primitive
plough. All the operations of the fields are beautiful
to see. They are beautiful in themselves and beautiful
in their suggestions of the permanence of things in
the midst of which we come and go like the guests
of a day. Who can see the gleaners in the field, or
the haymakers piling the hay on the hay-wain, or
the mower bending over the scythe without the stir-
ring of the feelings which the mere beauty of the
scene or of the motion does not explain? Indeed the
sense of beauty itself is probably only the emanation
of the thoughts subtly awakened by the action. It is
so with pictures. I do not know any painting that
lives in my mind with a more abiding beauty than
one of Millet's. It is just a solitary upland field, with

October Days

a flight of birds and an untended plough lying in the foreground. The barrenness and austerity of the scene are almost forbidding at the first glance, but as the mind dwells on it, it becomes instinct with meaning and emotion. Evening has come and darkness is falling over the land. The labourer has left the field and the rooks are going home. In the midst of the ancient solitude and silence that have taken possession of the earth, the old plough has the passion of personality. It embodies the epic of man's labour with the intensity that direct statement could not convey but only the power of suggestion can give.

And so it is with the scene before me. As I watch the ploughman drawing that straight, undulating line in the yellow stubble of the field, he seems to be not so much a mortal as a part of the landscape, that comes and goes as the seasons come and go, or as the sun comes and goes. His father, it may be, ploughed this field before him, and his father before him, and so on back through the centuries to the days when the monks still drank their sack and ate their venison in the monastery below, which is now only a mound of stones. And over the new-ploughed soil the rooks, who have as ancient an ancestry as himself, descend in clouds to forage as they have descended in these late October days for a thousand years. And after the rooks, the starlings. They have gathered in hosts after the pleasant domestic intimacies of summer for their winter campaigning, and stream across the sky in those miraculous mass manœuvres that affect one like winged and noiseless music. When they swoop down on the upturned soil the farmer blesses them.

October Days

He forgets the devastations of the summer in the presence of the ruthless war which the mail-clad host is making on the leather-jackets and other pestilent broods that lurk in the soil. They, too, have their part in the eternal economy of the fields. They are notes in that rhythm of things which touches our transitoriness with the hint of immemorial ancestry.

The ploughman has reached the far end of his furrow and rests his horses while he takes his lunch by the hedgerow. That is aflame once more with the returning splendours of these October days. The green of summer has turned to a passion of gold and scarlet and yellow and purple, and all over the landscape the foliage is drunk with colour. The elms that have stood so long garbed in sober green are showing wonderful tufts and curls of bright yellow at the top, like old gentlemen who are growing old gaily. It is as though they have suddenly become vocal and hilarious and are breaking into song. A few days hence they will be a glory of bright yellow. But that last note of triumph does not belong to October. It is in the first days of November that the elm is at its crowning hour. But the beech is at its best now, and the woodlands that spread up the hillside glow, underfoot and overhead, with the fires of fairyland.

In the bright warm sunshine there is a faint echo of the songs of spring. There are chirrups and chatterings from voices that have been silent for long. There is the "spink, spink" of the chaffinch, and from the meadowland at the back there comes at intervals the song of a lark, not the full song of summer, but no mean imitation of it. It is the robin, however,

who is now chorister-in-chief. His voice was lost or
unnoticed when the great soloists were abroad, but
now he is left to sing the requiem of the year alone—
unless we include the owl who comes punctually
every evening as the dusk falls to my garden, and
utters a few owlish incantations.

I can see the ploughman nearing the top end of
the field, and can hear the jangle of the harness and
his comments to the horses and almost the soft fall
of the soil as the furrow is turned over. I think I will
bid him adieu, for these October days provide tasks
for me as well as for the ploughman. There are still
some apples to pick, there is an amazing bed of carrots
to be got up, there are laurels to be cut down, there
are—oh, joy!—bonfires to be lighted, and there are
young fir-trees to be transplanted. I think I will
start with the bonfires.

THE END